How to Get Rid of "it"

Before "it" Gets Rid of You

Topical Handbook for Healing and Deliverance from Domestic Problems

A Practical Self-Help Guide to Spiritual and Personal Growth

A series of easy spiritual exercises, interactive tools,
And step-by-step instructions to receive
Freedom from bondage
And experience spiritual healing and deliverance

Volume Eleven

ISBN-13: 978-1986461818

ISBN-10: 1986461815

TAYLOR MADE
PUBLISHER

How to Get Rid of "it"

Before "it" Gets Rid of You

Topical Handbook for Healing and Deliverance from Domestic Problems

A Practical Self-Help Guide to Spiritual and Personal Growth

A series of easy spiritual exercises, interactive tools,
And step-by-step instructions to receive
Freedom from bondage
And experience spiritual healing and deliverance

Volume Eleven

Compilations of Works
By
Dr. Paulette Douglas

DEDICATION

**This book is dedicated to my Loving,
Supportive, Faithful Family, Friends, Mentors and Mentees**

I have always had many wonderful people to inspirer me to be the Women that God has ordained me to be and to continue to minister to God's people and to make full proof of my ministry

CONTENT

PREFACE

How to Get Rid of "it", Before "it" Gets Rid of You is a Deliverance and Spiritual Warfare Manual compiled by Dr. Paulette Douglas which is worth reading and re-reading more than once, in order to empower the reader when confronting personal crisis and trials. Dr. Paulette Douglas has compiled many practical, spiritual books bringing light to the evil that exists. She brings the deliverance ministry to the forefront, explaining how each and every believer can counteract evil and the devil. Not many believers understand the concept of the Holy Spirit and that we are all called to fight against the devil, our enemy. Dr. Paulette Douglas presents scriptural background and Bible passages from the old and new testaments, as well as prayers to share with the reader that each of us is called to resist and fight against the devil with the power of the Holy Spirit. Dr. Paulette Douglas refers to this as the deliverance ministry and explains this is one of the privileges all believers have at our disposal.

This background scripture material is necessary as many readers may be unfamiliar with these spiritual concepts. The main focus on the book is to be a manual; or one stop guide to show the reader what the bible has to say about deliverance as well as to expose the works and deceptions of the devil as well. The cover itself might seem an actual handbook- yet this book is truly a manual for deliverance. This exhaustive book contains too much information to be digested in a single, quick reading. The words contained are life changing. While some traditional readers and those in organized religion may find this book difficult to believe and a bit theatrical, a close-minded attitude is exactly what the devil wants in order to operate.

It is important to keep in mind the charismatic background of Dr. Paulette Douglas is based on the belief of the real workings of the Holy Spirit and the literal belief in modern day spiritual gifts such as tongues and healing. Much of the book is an invaluable resource where Dr. Douglas has taken scriptural truths and prayers and relates them to the modern-day believer to use and apply when facing any trial or work from the enemy. The scriptural references will empower any reader with a quick resource of how to respond in faith to any difficulty- large and small. It is a spiritual self-help book in the fact that it will allow the reader the tools to look within himself/her-self and identify any areas or issues where Satan has his foothold. Not only that it tells the reader how to face and address these issues! For those who are at a loss of how to begin to approach their spiritual problems there are a number of sample prayers applicable to any number of situations. The reader will get the impression as if this book was written for his or her own situation. This is a book to meditate on and use- and is not intended to collect dust on a book shelf. There are eleven sequels to this handbook which address many other issues that just might cover your "it".

In this twelve-book series, How to Get Rid of "it" Before "it" gets Rid of You we discuss evil spirits and how they operate:
1. The Apostolic anointing and ministry
2. How demons enter and oppress people
3. Curses and how to deal with them
4. Breaking bondages
5. Casting out spirits
6. Healing the wounded heart

7. Ungodly beliefs
8. Ministering to people
9. House cleansing
10. Discerning of spirits

In this volume we deal with the root causes of the "it' of domestic problems and How to get rid of the "it" of domestic problems before it gets rid of you. Domestic problems is something what plagues many people today, whether salvation issues related to food, sex, drugs, alcohol, smoking, spending, masturbation, porn, etc. Some inexperienced deliverance ministers might go after a spirit of domestic problems, which may bring freedom, but often, it doesn't bring lasting freedom. Many times, there is a root that needs to be pulled up, alongside casting out any residing spirits that are holding the person in bondage to domestic problems. Getting to the root of salvation issues is the key to bringing a person lasting genuine freedom. I am going to address the most common roots to domestic problems, and hopefully give you an idea of how this bondage works so that you can minister lasting freedom to this type of bondage.

INTRODUCTION

"It Is Finished"
The Words of Victory

"When Jesus therefore had received the vinegar, he said, "It is finished."—John 19:30
Words of triumph. In His words, "My God, my God, why hast thou forsaken me?" we heard the
Savior's cry of desolation. In His words, "I thirst" we listened to His cry of lamentation. Now
there falls upon our ears His cry of jubilation— "It is finished." From the words of the victim we
turn now to the words of the Victor. The Cross of Christ has two great sides to it: it showed the
profound depths of His humiliation, but it also marked the goal of the Incarnation, and further, it
told the consummation of His mission, and it forms the basis of our salvation.

It is finished." What is found in these three words, "It is finished" is wrapped up the Gospel of
God. In these words, contained the ground of the believer's assurance. In those words, is
discovered the sum of all joy, and the very spirit of all divine consolation. Every" it" that we
could ever encounter in our lives was dealt with on the cross therefore; we have the victory
through Jesus Christ over any and every "it".

"It is finished." This was not the despairing cry of a helpless martyr. It was not an expression of
satisfaction that the termination of His sufferings was now reached. It was not the last gasp of a
worn-out life. No, rather was it the declaration on the part of the divine Redeemer that all for
which He came from heaven to earth to do, was now done; that all that was needed to reveal the
full character of God had now been accomplished; that all that was required by the Law before
sinners could be saved, had now been performed—that the full price of our redemption was now
paid.

"It is finished." The great purpose of God in the history of man was now accomplished—from
the beginning, God's purpose has always been one and indivisible. It had been declared to men
in numerous ways: in symbol and type, by mysterious hints and by plain intimations, through
Messianic prediction and through didactic declaration. That purpose of God may be summarized
thus: to display His grace in the creating of children in His own image and glory. And at the
Cross the foundation was laid which was to make this possible and actual.

"It is finished." What was finished? The answer to this question is a very full one, though many
excellent expositors have sought to limit the scope of these words and to confine them strictly to
a single application. We are told it was the prophecies concerning the sufferings of Jesus which
were finished, and that He referred only to this. It is readily granted that the immediate reference
was to the Messianic predictions, yet we think there are good and sufficient reasons for not
confining our Lord's words here to them. Yea, to us it seems certain that Christ referred specially
to His sacrificial work, for all Scripture concerning His suffering and shame was not yet fulfilled.
There remained the dismissal of His spirit into the hands of the Father (Psa 31:5); there remained
the "piercing" with the spear (Zec 12:10: and note that the word used in Psalm 22:16 for the
piercing of His hands and feet—the act of crucifixion—is a different one); there still remained

the preserving of His bones unbroken (Psa 34:20), and the burial in the rich man's grave (Isa 53:9).

"It is finished." What was finished? We answer His sacrificial work. It is true there yet remained the act of death itself, which was necessary for the making of atonement. But, as is so often the case here in John's Gospel wherein our text is found (cf. Joh 12:23, 31; 13:31; 16:5; 17:4), the Lord here speaks of the completion of His work. Moreover, it must be remembered that the three hours darkness was already past, the awful cup had already been drained, His precious blood had already been shed, the outpoured wrath of God had already been endured; and these are the primary elements in the making of propitiation. The sacrificial work of Jesus, then, was completed, excepting only the act of death which followed immediately. But, as we shall see, the completing of the sacrificial work made an end of several things.

"It is finished."
1. Here we see the accomplished fulfillment of all the prophecies which had been written of Him here He should die. This is the immediate thought of the context: "When Jesus therefore had received the vinegar, He said, It is finished" (John 19:30). Centuries beforehand, the prophets of God had described step by step the humiliation and suffering which the coming Savior should undergo. One by one these had been fulfilled, wonderfully fulfilled, fulfilled to the very letter. Had prophecy declared that He should be the "woman's seed" (Gen 3:15), then He was "born of a woman" (Gal 4:4). Had prophecy announced that His mother should be a "virgin" (Isa 7:14), then was it literally fulfilled (Mat 1:18). Had prophecy revealed that He should be of the seed of Abraham (Gen 22:18), then mark its fulfillment (Mat 1:1). Had prophecy made it known that He

Prophecy said that He should be named before He was born (Isa 49:1), then so it came to pass (Luke 1:30-31). Had prophecy foretold that He should be born in Bethlehem of Judea (Mic 5:2), then mark how this very village was His birthplace. Had prophecy forewarned that His birth should entail sorrowing for others (Jer 31:15), then behold its tragic fulfillment (Mat 2:14-18). Had prophecy foreshown that the Messiah should appear before the scepter of tribal ascendancy had departed from Judah (Gen 49:10), then so He did, for though the ten tribes were in captivity, Judah was still in the land at the time of His advent. Had prophecy referred to the flight into Egypt and the subsequent return into Palestine, (Hose 11:1 and cf. Isa 49:3, 6), then so it came to pass (Mat 2:1415).

Prophecy made mention of one going before Christ to make ready His way (Mal 3:1), then see its fulfillment in the person of John the Baptist. Had prophecy made it known that at the Messiah's appearing "the eyes of the blind shall be opened, and the ears of the deaf shall be unstopped, then shall the lame man leap as a hart, and the tongue of the dumb sing" (Isa 35:56), then read through the four Gospels and see how blessedly this proved true. Had prophecy spoken of Him as "poor and needy" (Psa 40:17, see beginning of Psalm), then behold Him not having where to lay His head. Had prophecy intimated that He should speak in "parables" (Psa 78:2), then such was frequently His method of teaching. Had prophecy depicted Him stilling the tempest (Psa 107:29), then this is exactly what He did. Had prophecy heralded His "triumphal entry" into Jerusalem (Zec 9:9), then so it came to pass!

Prophecy announced that His person should be despised (Isa 53:3), that He should be rejected by the Jews (Isa 8:14), that He should be "hated without a cause" (Psa 69:4), then sad to say, such was precisely the case. Had prophecy painted the whole picture of His degradation and crucifixion, then was it vividly reproduced. There had been the betrayal by a familiar friend, the forsaking by His disciples, the being led to the slaughter, the being taken to judgment, the appearing of false witnesses against Him, the refusal on His part to make defense, the establishing of His innocence, the unjust condemnation, the sentence of capital punishment passed upon Him, the literal piercing of His hands and feet, the being numbered with transgressors, the mockery of the crowd, the casting lots for His garments—all predicted centuries beforehand, and all fulfilled to the very letter. The last prophecy of all which remained here He committed His Spirit into the hands of His Father, had now been fulfilled. He cried "I thirst," and after the tendering of the vinegar and gall, all was now "accomplished"; and as the Lord Jesus reviewed the entire scope of the prophetic Word and saw its full realization, He cried,

"It is finished"!
It only remains for us to point out that as there was a complete set of prophecies which had to do with the first advent of Jesus, so also is there a complete set of prophecies which have to do with His second advent—the latter as definite, as personal, and as comprehensive in their scope as the former. As then we see the actual fulfillment of those which had to do with His first coming to the earth, we may look forward with absolute confidence and assurance to the fulfillment of those which have to do with His second coming. And, as we have seen that the former set of prophecies were fulfilled literally and personally, so also must we expect the latter set to be. To grant the literal fulfillment of the former, and then to seek to spiritualize and symbolize the latter, is not only grossly inconsistent and illogical, but is highly injurious to us and deeply dishonoring to God and to His Word.

"It is finished."
2. Here we see the completion of His sufferings. But what tongue or pen can describe the sufferings of Jesus? The anguish, physical, mental, and spiritual, which He endured! Appropriately was He designated "the man of sorrows": suffering at the hands of men, at the hands of Satan, and at the hands of God. Pain inflicted upon Him by enemies and friends alike. From the beginning He walked the shadows which the Cross cast His path. "I am afflicted and ready to die from my youth up" (Psa 88:15). What a light this throws on His earlier years! Who can say how much is contained in those words? For us, an impenetrable veil is cast over the future; none of us knows what a day may bring forth.

But Jesus knew the end from the beginning! One has only to read through the Gospels to learn how the awful Cross was ever before Him. At the marriage-feast of Cana, where all was gladness and merriment, He makes solemn reference to "his hour" not yet come. When Nicodemus interviewed Him at night, the Savior referred to the "lifting up of the Son of man." When James and John came to request from Him the two places of honor in His coming kingdom, He made mention of the "cup" which He had to drink, and of the "baptism" wherewith He must be baptized. When Peter confessed that He was the Christ, the Son of the living God, He turned to His disciples and began to show unto them "how that he must go unto Jerusalem, and suffer many things of the elders and chief priests and scribes, and be killed, and be raised again the third day" (Mat 16:21). When Moses and Elijah stood with Him on the Mount of Transfiguration, it was to speak of "his decease which he should accomplish at Jerusalem" (Luke 9:31).

If it is true we are quite unable to estimate the sufferings of Christ due to the anticipation of the Cross, still less can we fathom the dread reality itself. The physical sufferings were excruciating, but even this was as nothing compared with His anguish of soul. To a consideration of these sufferings we have already devoted several paragraphs in previous chapters, yet we make no apology in turning to them again. We cannot contemplate too often what Jesus endured to secure our salvation. The better we are acquainted with His sufferings, and the more frequently we meditate thereon, the warmer will be our love and the deeper our gratitude.
At last the closing hours have come. There had been the terrible experience in Gethsemane followed by the appearing before Caiaphas, before Pilate, before Herod, and back again before Pilate. There had been the scourging and mocking by the brutal soldiers; the journey to Calvary; the fastening of His hands and feet to the cruel tree. There had been the reviling of the priests, the crowd, and the two thieves crucified with Him.

There had been the awful cloud that hid from the Father's face, which wrung from Him the bitter cry, "My God, my God, why hast thou forsaken me?" There had been the parched lips which drew from Him the exclamation "I thirst." There had been the fearful conflict with the power of darkness as the serpent "bruised" His heel. But now the suffering is ended. The Lord has bruised Him; man, and Devil have done their worst. The cup has been drained. The awful storm of God's wrath has spent itself. The darkness is ended. The sword of divine justice is done. The wages of sin have been paid. The prophecies of His sufferings are all fulfilled. The Cross has been "endured." Divine holiness has been fully satisfied (Isa 53:11). With a cry of triumph—a loud cry, a cry which reverberated throughout the entire universe—Jesus exclaims, "It is finished." The shame, the suffering and agony, are past. Never again shall He experience pain. Never again shall He endure the contradiction of sinners against Himself. Never again shall He be in the hands of Satan. Never again shall the light of God's countenance be hidden from Him. Blessed be God, all that is finished! "It is finished."

Jesus is concerned in the work of Redemption: He was the One who came here to die for sinners. He is the One who now gives spiritual illumination and understanding, and guides into the truth. Before the Lord Jesus came to this earth, a definite work was committed to Him. In the volume of the book it was written of Him, and He came to do the recorded will of God. Even as a boy of twelve the "Father's business" was before His heart and occupied His attention. Again, in John 5:36 we find Him saying, "But I have greater witness than that of John: for the works which the Father hath given me to finish, the same works that I do." And on the last night before His death, in that wonderful high priestly prayer, we find Him saying, "I have glorified thee on the earth: I have finished the work which thou gavest me to do" (John 17:4).

The mission upon which God had sent His Son into the world was now accomplished. It was not actually finished till He breathed His last, but death was only an instant ahead, and in anticipation of it He cries "It is finished." The demanding work is done. The divinely-given task is performed. A work more honorable and momentous than ever entrusted to man or angels, has been completed. That for which He had left heaven's glory that for which He had taken upon Him the form of a servant, that for which He had remained upon earth for thirty-three years to do, was now consummated. Nothing remained to be added. The goal of the Incarnation is reached. With what joyous triumph must He here have viewed the costly work which, committed to Him, had now been perfected!

"It is finished." The mission upon which God had sent His Son into the world was accomplished. That which had been eternally purposed had come to pass. The plan of God had been fully carried out.

Because He is the Most High, God's will, cannot be thwarted. Because He is supreme, God's counsel must stand. Because He is almighty, God's purpose cannot be overthrown.

"But he is in one mind, and who can turn him? And what his soul desireth, even that he doeth" (Job 23:13). "I know that thou canst do everything, and that no thought can be withholding from thee" (Job 42:2). "But our God is in the heavens: He hath done whatsoever he hath pleased" (Psa 115:3). "There is no wisdom nor understanding nor counsel against the Lord" (Pro 21:30). "For the Lord of hosts hath purposed, and who shall disannul it? And His hand is stretched out, and who shall turn it back?" (Isa 14:27). "Remember the former things of old: for I am God, and there is none else; I am God, and there is none like me: Declaring the end from the beginning, and from ancient times the things that are not yet done, saying, My counsel shall stand, and I will do all my pleasure" (Isa 46:9-10). "And all the inhabitants of the earth are reputed as nothing: and he doeth according to his will in the army of heaven, and among the inhabitants of the earth: and none can stay his hand, or say unto him, What doest thou?" (Dan 4:35). And, in the triumphant cry of the Jesus— "It is finished"—we have a prophecy and pledge of the ultimate carrying out of God's plan completely. At the end of time, when everything is wound up, and God's purpose has been fully consummated, when everything has been done which He before determined should be done, then shall it be said again, "It is finished."

"It is finished."

4. Here we see the accomplishment of the Atonement. Above we have spoken of Christ reaching the goal of the Incarnation, and of the consummation of His mission to the earth; what that goal and mission was, the Scriptures plainly reveal. The Son of Man came here "to seek and to save that which was lost" (Luke 19:10). Christ Jesus came into the world "to save sinners" (1Ti 1:15). God sent forth His Son, born of a woman, "to redeem them that were under the law" (Gal 4:5). He was manifested "to take away our sins" (1Jo 3:5). And all this involved the Cross. The "lost" which He came to seek could only be found there—in the place of death and under the condemnation of God. Sinners could be "saved" only by One taking their place and bearing their iniquities. They who were under the Law could be "redeemed" only by Another fulfilling its requirements and suffering its curse. Our sins could be "taken away" only by their being blotted out by the precious blood of Christ. The demands of justice must be met; the requirements of God's holiness must be satisfied; the awful debt we incurred must be paid. And on the Cross, this was done; done by none less than the Son of God; done perfectly; done once for all.

"It is finished."

That to which so many types looked forward, was now accomplished. A covering from sin and its shame, typified by the coats of skin with which the Lord God clothed our first parents, was now provided. The more excellent sacrifice, typified by Abel's lamb, had now been offered. A shelter from the storm of divine judgment, typified by the Ark of Noah, was now furnished. The only-begotten and well-beloved Son, typified by Abraham's offering up of Isaac, had already been placed upon the altar. A protection from the avenging angel, typified by the shed blood of the Passover-lamb, was now supplied. A cure from the serpent's bite, typified by the serpent of brass upon the pole, was now made ready for sinners. The providing of a life-giving fountain, typified by Moses striking the rock, was now affected.

"It is finished." The Greek word here, teleo, is translated variously in the New Testament. A glance at some of the different renderings in other passages will enable us to discern the fullness and finality of the term used by Jesus. In Matthew 11:1, teleo is rendered as follows, "When Jesus had made an end of commanding his twelve disciples, he departed thence." In Matthew 17:24 it is rendered, "They that received tribute money came to Peter, and said, Doth not your master pay tribute?" In Luke 2:39, it is rendered, "And when they had performed all things according to the Law of the Lord, they returned into Galilee." In Luke 18:31, it is rendered, "All things that are written by the prophets concerning the Son shall be accomplished."

"It is finished." He cried: it is "made an end of"; it is "paid"; it is "performed"; it is "accomplished." What was made an end of? —our sins and their guilt. What was "paid?"—the price of our redemption. What was "performed?"—the utmost requirements of the Law. What was "accomplished?"—the work which the Father had given Him to do. What was "finished?"— the making of atonement. God has furnished at least four proofs that Christ did finish the work which was given Him to do. First, in the rending of the veil, which showed that the way to God was now open. Second, in the raising of Christ from the dead, which evidenced that God had accepted His sacrifice. Third, the exaltation of Christ to His own right hand, which demonstrated the value of Christ's work and the Father's delight in His person. Fourth, the sending to earth of the Holy Spirit to apply the virtues and benefits of Christ's atoning death.

"It is finished." What was "finished?"—the work of atonement. What is the value of that to us? This: to the sinner, it is a message of glad tidings. All that a Holy God requires has been done. Nothing is left for the sinner to add. No works from us are demanded as the price of our salvation. All that is necessary for the sinner is to rest now by faith upon what Christ did. "The gift of God is eternal life through Jesus Christ our Lord" (Rom 6:23). To the believer, the knowledge that the atoning work of Christ is finished brings a sweet relief over against all the defects and imperfections of his services. There is nothing "finished" that we do: all our duties are imperfect. There is much of sin and vanity in the very best of our efforts, but the grand relief is that we are "complete" in Christ (Col 2:10)! Christ and His finished work are the ground of all our hopes. "It is finished."

5. Here we see the end of our sins. The sins of the believer, all of them, were transferred to the Jesus. As the Scripture says, "The Lord hath laid on him the iniquities of us all" (Isa 53:6). If then God laid my iniquities on Christ, they are no longer on me. Sin there is in me, for the old Adamic nature remains in the believer till death or till Christ's return, should He come before I die; but there is no sin on me. This distinction between sin in and sin on, is a vital one, and there should be little difficulty in apprehending it. If I were to say the judge passed sentence on a criminal, and that he is now under sentence of death, everyone would understand what I meant. In like manner, everyone out of Christ has the sentence of God's condemnation resting upon him. But when a sinner believes in the Lord Jesus, and receives Him as his Lord and Master, obey the salvation message according to (Acts 2:38-39) he is no longer "under condemnation"— sin is no longer on him, that is, the guilt, the condemnation, the penalty of sin, is no longer upon

him. And why? Because Christ bore our sins in His own body on the tree (1Pe 2:24)—the guilt, condemnation, and penalty of our sins, was transferred to our substitute. Hence, because my sins were transferred to Christ, they are no more upon me.

This precious truth was strikingly illustrated in Old Testament times regarding Israel's annual Day of Atonement. On that day, Aaron, the high priest (a type of Christ), made satisfaction to God for the sins which Israel had committed during the previous year. The way this was done is described in Leviticus 16. Two goats were taken and presented before the Lord at the door of the tabernacle: this was before anything was done with them: it represented Christ being sent and presenting Himself, offering to come into this world and be the Savior of sinners. One of the goats was then taken and killed, and its blood was carried into the tabernacle, within the veil, into the Holy of Holies, and there it was sprinkled before and upon the mercy seat—foreshadowing Christ offering Himself as a sacrifice, to meet the demands of His justice and satisfy the requirements of His holiness.

Then we read that Aaron came out of the tabernacle and laid both his hands upon the head of the second (living) goat— signifying an act of identification by which Aaron is the representative of the whole nation, identified the people with it, acknowledging that its doom was what their sins merited, and which, today, corresponds with the hands of faith laying hold of Christ and identifying ourselves with Him in His Death. Having laid his hands on the head of the live goat, Aaron now confessed over him "all the iniquities of the children of Israel, and all their transgressions in all their sins, putting them upon the head of the goat" (Lev 16:21). Thus, were Israel's sins transferred to their substitute. Finally, we are told, "And the goat shall bear upon him all their iniquities unto a land not inhabited: and he shall let go the goat in the wilderness" (Lev 16:22). The goat bearing Israel's sins, was taken unto an uninhabited wilderness, and the people of God saw him and their sins no more! In type this was Christ taking our sins into that desolate land where God was not and there making an end of them. The Cross of Christ then is the grave of our sins!

"It is finished."
6. Here we see the fulfillment of the Law's requirements. "The law is holy, and the commandment holy, and just and good" (Rom 7:12). How could it be anything less when Jehovah Himself had framed and given it! The fault lay not in the Law but in man who, being depraved and sinful, could not keep it. Yet that Law must be kept, and kept by a man, so that the Law might be honored and magnified, and its giver vindicated. Therefore, we read, "For what the law could not do, in that it was weak through the flesh, God sending his own Son, in the likeness of sinful flesh, and for sin, condemned sin in the flesh: that the righteousness of the law might be fulfilled in [not by] us, who walk not after flesh, but after the Spirit" (Rom 8:3-4). The "weakness" here is that of fallen man. The sending forth of God's Son in the likeness of sin's flesh (Greek) refers to the Incarnation: as we read in another Scripture, "God sent forth his Son, born of a woman, born under the law, that he might redeem them that were under the law" (Gal 4:4-5 RV). Yes, the Jesus was born "under the law," born under it that He might keep it perfectly in thought, word, and deed. "Think not that I am come to destroy the law, or the prophets: I am not come to destroy, but to fulfill" (Mat 5:17); such was His claim.

But not only did Jesus keep the precepts of the Law, He also suffered its penalty and endured its curse. We had broken it, and taking our place, He must receive its just sentence. Having received its penalty and endured its curse, the demands of the Law are fully met, and justice is satisfied. Therefore, is it written of believers, "Christ hath redeemed us from the curse of the law, being made a curse for us" (Gal 3:13). And again, "For Christ is the end of the law for righteousness to everyone that believeth" (Rom 10:4). And yet again, "For ye are not under the law, but under grace" (Rom 6:14). "It is finished." "Free from the Law, Jesus hath bled, and there is remission, cursed by the law and bruised by the fall, Grace hath redeemed us once for all."

7. Here we see the destruction of Satan's power. See it by faith. The Cross sounded the death of the devil's power. To human appearances it looked like the moment of his greatest triumph, yet, it was the hour of his ultimate defeat. In view of the Cross Jesus declared, "Now is the judgment of this world: now shall the prince of this world be cast out" (Joh 12:31). It is true that Satan has not yet been chained and cast into the bottomless pit, nevertheless, sentence has been passed (though not yet executed); his doom is certain; and his power is already broken so far as believers are concerned.

For the Christian, the devil is a vanquished foe. He was defeated by Christ at the Cross— "that through death he might destroy him that had the power of death, that is, the devil" (Hebrew 2:14). Believers have already been "delivered from the power of darkness" and translated into the kingdom of God's dear Son (Col 1:13). Satan, then, should be treated as a defeated enemy. No longer has he any legitimate claim upon us. Once we were his lawful "captives"; but now God worketh in us both to will and to do of His good pleasure. All that we now must do is to "resist the devil," and the promise is, "he will flee from you" (James 4:7).

"It is finished." Here was the triumphant answer to the rage of man and the enmity of Satan. It tells of the perfect work which meets sin in the place of judgment. All was completed just as God would have it, just as the prophets had foretold, just as the Old Testament ceremonial had foreshadowed, just as divine holiness demanded, and just as sinners needed. How strikingly appropriate is this sixth Cross-utterance of Jesus found in John's Gospel—the Gospel which displays the glory of Christ's deity! He seals it with His own words, attesting it is complete, and giving it the all-sufficient sanction of His own approval. Jesus says, "It is finished"—who then dare doubt or question it.

"It is finished." Reader, do you believe it? or, are you trying to add something of your own to the finished work of Christ to secure the favor of God? All you must do is to accept the pardon which He purchased. God is satisfied with His work on the cross, why are not you? Sinner, the moment you believe Jesus' testimony that it is finished, that moment every sin you have committed is blotted out, and you stand accepted in Christ! O would you not like to possess the assurance that there is nothing between your soul and God? Would you not like to know that every sin had been atoned for and put away? Then believe what God's Word says about Christ's death. Rest not on your feelings and experiences but on the written Word. There is only one way of finding peace, deliverance, wholeness, salvation, victory over the "it" and that is through faith in the shed blood of Jesus the of Lamb God. It is time to "Get Rid of "it", Before "it" Gets Rid of You".

"It is finished." Do you really believe it? Or, are you endeavoring to add something of your own to it and thus merit the favor of God? By continuing to hold on and struggle, seeking other sources to deal with the "it" in your life, you are nullifying the finished work of Christ by your own miserable additions to it!". The Gospel of God's grace, and the finished work of Christ is sufficient for our souls to rest upon. In the pages of this book, God uses forceful object lessons and His Word to show you, "How to Get Rid of "it", before "it" Gets Rid of You". It is a grave mistake not to embrace the Word of God, and cast yourself by faith upon what Christ had done for you.

Victory was given to us by way of the cross. Whatever your "it" or "its" might be, "it" has come to kill, steal and destroy you. Make a conscious effort to explore this information given in this book and expose the enemy of your soul. Let's "Get Rid of "it". After all, "It is Finished"

CHAPTER ONE

What is "it"?

We are all created with a basic need to be loved. God created us to both give and receive love, but though damaged emotions, our capacity to receive love can be dramatically hindered. Ignorance of God's love will also hinder us from receiving the great and glorious love that He has for us. **The root of most "its" is a lack of love being received by that person.** Many of us have been damaged emotionally by rejection, abandonment, abuse, etc., and thereby our capacity to receive love has been reduced. **Only an emotionally healthy person is capable of both giving and receiving love as God intended.**

Self-worth issues can hinder love

Self-worth issues are rooted in believing that we are not worthy or deserve to be loved. When we believe that we are unlovable, we will unconsciously reject any love that comes our way. We won't believe the love, because we believe in our hearts that we are not worthy. **Self-worth issues are all rooted in our failing to see who we really are in Christ.**

If you walked into a gallery of world-class art, and pointed to a painting, saying, "That is the ugliest thing I've ever seen! Who painted that??" Now let's say the artist was standing right next to you. How do you think that would make him feel? Do you realize we are the artwork of God, a special painting crafted together by the master painter? Do you think it brings Him honor when we look down on ourselves? **We need to stop putting down what God has made.**

Many times, we have self-unforgiveness issues because we blame ourselves for something, or we've done something we deeply regret, and we simply cannot let it go. We need to realize that Jesus has forgiven us of all our failures, and we need to start seeing ourselves as forgiven. Otherwise, we're denying the work of Christ in our life! **If God forgave you, and you're still beating yourself up, then you don't really believe what Jesus did for you.** It's that simple!

Just as we must forgive others (see Matthew 18:21-35), we need to forgive ourselves just the same. Self-hate has been known to be the root behind diseases such as lupus and Crohn's disease, as well as other auto-immune diseases. We need to stop holding ourselves accountable for that which Jesus has set us free from.

If we want to be in faith, we need to BELIEVE what Jesus did for us, and part of that believing is seeing ourselves as forgiven and clothed with the righteousness of God,

16

which is upon all who believe in the finished work of Christ. Without faith, it is impossible to please God (see Hebrews 11:6), so if you want to please God, start taking the finished work of the cross seriously, and begin to see yourself as forgiven, washed clean, and clothed in the righteousness of God. For the righteousness (right standing with God) is upon all who believe:

> *"Even the righteousness of God which is by faith of Jesus Christ unto all and upon all them that believe..." (Romans 3:22 KJV)*

Unforgiveness is rooted in a lack of realization of how much God has forgiven us, and therefore we're not thankful for the steep and terrible price that Jesus paid for our own failures. Therefore, it is so important to mediate on what Jesus did for us, until it transforms our heart. The message of Jesus' work for us is what causes faith to arise in our hearts and transforms us from the inside out (read Romans 10:8-17).

Learning to see yourself as God sees you, and forgive yourself because you want to please God and be in faith and be thankful for what Jesus did for you, is the biggest step in overcoming self-worth issues. Of course, there are spirits that may need to be driven out as well, such as self-hate, guilt, condemnation, etc.

Receiving the love God has for us

When it comes to God's love for us, that's obvious, considering how He loves even the sinner so much that Jesus came to die for them. Anybody who knows the message of the cross, has some knowledge of God's love for us. However, many times, we blame God for our problems, and so we don't believe the love that He has for us. Not only do we blame Him for our problems, many times we think that God gave us the sickness or problem in our life to teach us something. Nothing could be further from the truth! Jesus tells us clearly who came to kill, steal, and destroy, and who came so that we could have life and have it in abundance.

> *"The thief cometh not, but for to steal, and to kill, and to destroy: I am come that they might have life, and that they might have it more abundantly." (John 10:10 KJV)*

If we are going to receive the love that God has for us, we need to get our thinking straightened out. He's not the one behind our problems, but rather Jesus paid the full price so that we can be forgiven all our sins, both physically and emotionally healed, and blessed.

> *"When the even was come, they brought unto him many that were possessed with devils: and he cast out the spirits with his word, and healed all that were*

sick: That it might be fulfilled which was spoken by Esaias the prophet, saying, Himself took our infirmities, and bare our sicknesses." (Matthew 8:16-17 KJV)

Look at how good God's heart is toward mankind! Not only did Jesus heal them, but He proved the blessings of the covenant we have with Him today concerning our healing and deliverance. Isn't He good toward us? **The reason why things happen to us, is because we live in a fallen world that is under the control of the evil one.** It's not God's fault. He loves you. Jesus died for you.

Settling the fact that God loves you and is good toward you is crucial to restoring your God-given capacity to receive His love. If you can't receive His love, then you need to stop and ask yourself four questions:

1. Am I blaming God for anything bad that happened to me?

2. Have I been emotionally wounded in such a way that it is hindering my ability to freely receive love as God intended me to?

3. Do I have knowledge and revelation of how much God loves me? Do I have a solid Biblical understanding of how I am loved with the same kind of love that the Father has for Jesus?

4. Is there a self-worth issue that makes me feel unworthy to be loved?

Settling these issues lays a foundation for breaking free from the power of the "IT". You must repair the damage and faulty thinking which hinders your ability to receive the love that God has for you.

How do you know if you are receiving God's love or if it's hindered? **If you are not passionate about Jesus, then somewhere your ability to receive His love is hindered.**

If you are living a life without receiving God's love in your heart daily, you are missing out on the most fulfilling life you can have here on this earth. To know God's love, which surpasses all understanding (see Philippians 4:7), dispels all our fears and gives us a sense of peace and joy that we could never otherwise know.

"And we have known and believed the love that God hath to us. God is love; and he that dwelleth in love dwelleth in God, and God in him. Herein is our love made perfect, that we may have boldness in the day of judgment: because as he is, so are we in this world. There is no fear in love; but perfect love casteth out fear: because fear hath torment. He that feareth is not made perfect in love." (1 John 4:16-18 KJV)

What exactly is "it"?

An "it" is formed when we try to use something other than God, to meet our need to be loved. When our ability to receive God's love into our hearts is hindered, we will feel like something is missing, and seek to fill that void with something else. When that thing, whatever it might be, fills that void, we grow to love "it" because it's meeting a need. Over time, we establish a relationship with that thing, and when it comes time to depart, it's like breaking up a relationship. That's why the "it" is so destructive; we've relied on that thing to meet a need and we've established a relationship with it. Now when it's time to break up the love, it isn't so easy to say goodbye.

One widespread problem that we see when we try to deal with "it", is where we give up one "it" successfully, only to find yourself with another "it". We might quit drinking only to start overeating, for example. We might think we're finding victory, but all we're really doing is trading one "it" for another "it". This is because something must fill the love-void in our hearts, and if it's not one thing, it will be another.

What about cutting or self-harm?

Cutting or self-mutation is a special type of "it", where there's a need to either release pain in a person's heart or the person believes that they deserve to be punished for their failures. In these cases, the person certainly has an issue receiving the love that God has for them but there's another type of root that needs to be addressed as well. There's emotional pain or guilt that the person is dealing with that needs to be resolved. Finding out what happened and receiving Christ's truth concerning those areas is important for their healing. Any bondage involving guilt will need to be resolved through realizing and accepting the work of Christ on the cross for that person and they will likely need spirits of guilt, condemnation, self-hate, etc. driven out in Jesus' name. Again, getting the person to see them self for who they really are in Christ, forgiven, loved, and blessed, is crucial to lasting freedom from self-hate issues.

See yourself as lovable!

The key in uprooting most "its" is to deal with the underlying issues which are limiting their capacity to freely receive love from God and others, along with dealing with any self-worth issues by establishing an understanding of your true identity in Christ. **Coming to a place where you believe you are lovable is key to receiving love in general**, so dealing with self-worth issues is an important key to breaking down the walls which keep us from feeling loved. The only way to obtain a true sense of worth and value is to get a revelation of how much you are loved by God, who sent His son Jesus to die for you.

Discovering the root

To discover the root of your "it", you need to get real honest with yourself. Many times, we are in denial about the pain we are feeling. Figuring out what is the root of a bondage is all about asking the right questions, and that is especially important when it comes to uprooting an "it". Why don't we feel loved? Do we feel unlovable? (Let's stop right there; if we feel unlovable, then you've just discovered a self-worth issue that will need to be addressed.) Are you passionate about Jesus? If not, then something in hindering you from realizing how much you are loved by Him who died for you. Do you see yourself as forgiven and loved by the God because of what He did for you?

As you discover emotional wounds, you'll need to forgive (others, yourself, and God) and invite Jesus to come and heal the damage in your heart. If you don't realize how much God loves you, then you'll need to spend some time learning about what Jesus did for you on the cross, and what a terrible price He paid because He loved you so very much. Often breaking out of an "it" is a combination of emotional healing, learning about who you are in Christ, forgiving (yourself, others, and God), overcoming self-worth issues by changing how you see yourself (in light of how God sees and loves you), and casting out any spirits that came in and are enforcing the destructive behavior. Spirits behind guilt, condemnation, etc. also need to be driven out, as they seek to keep us from fully seeing what Jesus did for us on the cross.

Dealing with the issues underlying an "it" is key to uprooting it permanently. If you want lasting freedom and wholeness in this area of your life, you will have to deal with the issues that have limited your capacity to receive love, especially the love that God has for you.

CHAPTER TWO

The "it" of Marriage Issues

DEFINITION: Biblically, marriage is the union of one man with one woman and the relationship that exists between them.

FACTS ABOUT MARRIAGE:

Fifty-percent of all marriages end in divorce. That is why it is important to deal with marriage problems before they intensify.

The biblical plan is that two people become one (Genesis 2:24). God intends for marriage to be between one man and one woman for life (Romans 7:2; 1 Corinthians 7:10-11; Jeremiah 32:19; Mark 10:9).

Be sure you marry "in the Lord." Believers are not to be unequally yoked together with unbelievers (1 Corinthians 7:39; 2 Corinthians 6:14). If you are already married to an unbeliever, you are to remain with them unless they decide to depart because it is possible that you will be able to win them to the Lord (1 Corinthians 7:15-16).

Do not marry someone in need of reform. The problems that you have with them now will only intensify. Marriage was not intended to be a "reform school."

Pre-marital checklist.
-Marriage should be only with the opposite sex--one man, one woman, for life: Genesis 2:18,22.
-You are required to cease dependence on your parents: Genesis 2:24.
-You must live together as one in legal and sexual union: Genesis 2:24.
-You must love and dwell with your partner for a lifetime: Mark 10:9.
-Believers must not marry unbelievers: 2 Corinthians 6:14-15,17.
-Be sure you have discussed and agreed on spiritual matters of faith, finances, communication, children, child discipline--every major area that will affect your union

Do not expect:
-Marriage to solve your personal problems.
-Religious differences to be insignificant.
-To change the attitudes, beliefs, or conduct of your spouse.
-That sexual passion alone will sustain your marriage.

Problems arise because of carnality.   Whether in the church, the home, or between friends and family members, problems arise because of carnality in the lives of believers (1 Corinthians 3:3). In a marriage, problems arise most frequent in the areas of sexual compatibility, in-law problems, finances, discipline of children, and spiritual issues.

A good marriage is based on God's will and His Word. Unless the Lord builds your marriage and your home, you are laboring in vain (Psalm 127:1).

A good marriage is based on basic tenets of respect for your mate, realistic expectations of one another, acceptance of your mate, and an ability to forgive. Good communication is vital to a good marriage, as is a genuine commitment to one another. Spiritual unity is most important.

God can heal all wounds. Whether it be a small misunderstanding or a major problem in a marriage, the Lord will heal your relationship if you will let Him (Jeremiah 30:17).

Note: Do not remain in a marriage where there is physical violence, child abuse, or illegal activities. Many innocent partners have suffered dire consequences because they did not remove themselves and their children from such environments--including violent death or criminal prosecution for not protecting their children.

DEALING WITH MARRIAGE:

Make a commitment to each other and to the relationship. Do not accept excuses for a poor relationship such as: "We never should have been married in the first place"; "Our families don't get along"; or "We have grown apart." All of these are issues that can be resolved on the basis of God's Word which mandates forgiving and being forgiven.

Seek the root cause of problems. What is causing the problems in your marriage? Is it unforgiveness, inability to accept each other, adultery, finances, problems with in-laws, spiritual disunity, disagreements over children, sexual incompatibility, communication problems, etc? These are some of the main problems in marriages. Deal with the root causes of the surface manifestations of marital unhappiness and disharmony.

Examine what you have done to try and solve these problems. Has what you have tried worked? Have you tried God's way--including forgiving one another, praying, and studying the Bible together so you can build your marriage on the Word of God?

Ask forgiveness. Seek forgiveness from God and from your spouse. If adultery was involved, the adulterous relationship must be totally severed by the offending party.

Pray together. Pray about your problems instead of fighting about them.

Study the Word of God together. All problems in marriage can be resolved by application of biblical principles. The question is, are you willing?

Attend church together. Find a Bible-believing church with a strong couples' ministry where you can continue to strengthen your marriage and establish biblical goals for your marriage.

Fellowship with couples who have strong marriages. Do not hang out with couples who fight and bicker. Develop relationships with those who model qualities of a positive marriage and learn from them.

Agree to these standards.
-We commit ourselves to live for God and allow Him to control our marriage.
-We commit to growing together spiritually.
-We commit our finances, communication, sex life, and children to the Lord and will follow His
  direction in each of these areas as well as every area of our lives.
-We will pray individually about a matter before we come together to talk about it.
-We will not discuss things in an angry, hostile, loud manner.
-We agree to hear the other person's opinion and accept alternate views.
-We will not go to bed angry.
-We agree to forgive--not dwelling on a past offense by continuing to bring it up.

WHAT GOD'S WORD SAYS ABOUT MARRIAGE:

Marriage relationships in general.

The Lord God said, "It is not good for the man to be alone. I will make a helper suitable for him." (Genesis 2:18)

The man said, "This is now bone of my bones and flesh of my flesh; she shall be called 'woman,' for she was taken out of man." For this reason, a man will leave his father and mother and be united to his wife, and they will become one flesh. (Genesis 2:23-24)

Unless the Lord builds the house, its builders labor in vain. (Psalm 127:1)

"You have heard that it was said, 'Do not commit adultery.' But I tell you that anyone who looks at a woman lustfully has already committed adultery with her in his heart." (Matthew 5:28)

"It has been said, 'Anyone who divorces his wife must give her a certificate of divorce.' But I tell you that anyone who divorces his wife, except for marital unfaithfulness, causes her to become an adulteress, and anyone who marries the divorced woman commits adultery. (Matthew 5:32)

"Why then," they asked, "did Moses command that a man give his wife a certificate of divorce and send her away?" Jesus replied, "Moses permitted you to divorce your wives because your hearts were hard. But it was not this way from the beginning. I tell you that anyone who divorces his wife, except for marital unfaithfulness, and marries another woman commits adultery." (Matthew 19:7-9)

But at the beginning of creation God made them male and female. For this reason a man will leave his father and mother and be united to his wife, and the two will become one flesh. So they

are no longer two, but one. Therefore, what God has joined together, let man not separate. (Mark 10:6-9)

You are still worldly. For since there is jealousy and quarreling among you, are you not worldly? Are you not acting like mere men? (1 Corinthians 3:3)

Do you not know that the wicked will not inherit the kingdom of God? Do not be deceived: Neither the sexually immoral nor idolaters nor adulterers nor male prostitutes nor homosexual offenders (1 Corinthians 6:9)

Flee from sexual immorality. All other sins a man commits are outside his body, but he who sins sexually sins against his own body. Do you not know that your body is a temple of the Holy Spirit, who is in you, whom you have received from God? You are not your own; you were bought at a price. Therefore, honor God with your body. (1 Corinthians 6:18-20)

A woman is bound to her husband as long as he lives. But if her husband dies, she is free to marry anyone she wishes, but he must belong to the Lord. (1 Corinthians 7:39)

Now I want you to realize that the head of every man is Christ, and the head of the woman is man, and the head of Christ is God. (1 Corinthians 11:3)

Do not be yoked together with unbelievers. For what do righteousness and wickedness have in common? Or what fellowship can light have with darkness? (2 Corinthians 6:14)

Marriage should be honored by all, and the marriage bed kept pure, for God will judge the adulterer and all the sexually immoral. (Hebrews 13:4)

Husbands.

Your wife will be like a fruitful vine within your house; your sons will be like olive shoots around your table. Thus, is the man blessed who fears the Lord. (Psalm 128:3-4)

He who finds a wife finds what is good and receives favor from the Lord. (Proverbs 18:22)

But I tell you that anyone who looks at a woman lustfully has already committed adultery with her in his heart. (Mathew 5:28)

But I tell you that anyone who divorces his wife, except for marital unfaithfulness, causes her to become an adulteress, and anyone who marries the divorced woman commits adultery. (Matthew 5:32)

Submit to one another out of reverence for Christ. Wives, submit to your husbands as to the Lord. For the husband is the head of the wife as Christ is the head of the church, his body, of which he is the Savior. Now as the church submits to Christ, so also wives should submit to their husbands in everything. Husbands, love your wives, just as Christ loved the church and gave himself up for her to make her holy, cleansing her by the washing with water through the word, and to present her to himself as a radiant church, without stain or wrinkle or any other blemish, but holy and blameless. In this same way, husbands ought to love their wives as their own bodies. He who loves his wife loves himself. After all, no one ever hated his own body, but he feeds and cares for it, just as Christ does the church--for we are members of his body. For this reason, a man will leave his father and mother and be united to his wife, and the two will become one flesh... However, each one of you also must love his wife as he loves himself, and the wife must respect her husband. (Ephesians 5:22-29, 33)

Husbands, love your wives and do not be harsh with them. (Colossians 3:19)

If any brother has a wife who is not a believer and she is willing to live with him, he must not divorce her... But if the unbeliever leaves, let him do so. A believing man or woman is not bound in such circumstances; God has called us to live in peace. How do you know, wife, whether you will save your husband? Or, how do you know, husband, whether you will save your wife? (1 Corinthians 7:12, 15-16)

Husbands, in the same way be considerate as you live with your wives, and treat them with respect as the weaker partner and as heirs with you of the gracious gift of life, so that nothing will hinder your prayers. (1 Peter 3:7)

Wives.

The Lord God said, "It is not good for the man to be alone. I will make a helper suitable for him." (Genesis 2:18)

Your desire will be for your husband, and he will rule over you. (Genesis 3:16)

A wife of noble character is her husband's crown, but a disgraceful wife is like decay in his bones. (Proverbs 12:4)

The wise woman builds her house, but with her own hands the foolish one tears hers down. (Proverbs 14:1)

Houses and wealth are inherited from parents, but a prudent wife is from the Lord. (Proverbs 19:14)

A quarrelsome wife is like a constant dripping. (Proverbs 19:13)

Better to live in a comer of the roof than share a house with a quarrelsome wife. (Proverbs 21:9)

Better to live in a desert than with a quarrelsome and ill-tempered wife. (Proverbs 21:19)

A quarrelsome wife is like a constant dripping on a rainy day; restraining her is like restraining the wind or grasping oil with the hand. (Proverbs 27:15-16)

Proverbs chapter 31: The model wife.

And if a woman has a husband who is not a believer and he is willing to live with her, she must not divorce him. For the unbelieving husband has been sanctified through his wife, and the unbelieving wife has been sanctified through her believing husband. Otherwise your children would be unclean, but as it is, they are holy. How do you know, wife, whether you will save your husband? Or, how do you know, husband, whether you will save your wife? (1 Corinthians 7:13-14,16)

Now I want you to realize that the head of every man is Christ, and the head of the woman is man, and the head of Christ is God. (1 Corinthians 11:3)

Wives, submit to your husbands as to the Lord. For the husband is the head of the wife as Christ is the head of the church, his body, of which he is the Savior. Now as the church submits to Christ, so also wives should submit to their husbands in everything. (Ephesians 5:22-24)

Wives, submit to your husbands, as is fitting in the Lord. (Colossians 3:18)

In the same way, their wives are to be women worthy of respect, not malicious talkers but temperate and trustworthy in everything. (1 Timothy 3:11)

So I counsel younger widows to marry, to have children, to manage their homes and to give the enemy no opportunity for slander. (1 Timothy 5:14)

So in everything, do to others what you would have them Wives, in the same way be submissive to your husbands so that, if any of them do not believe the word, they may be won over without words by the behavior of their wives, when they see the purity and reverence of your lives. (1 Peter 3:1-2)

Your beauty should not come from outward adornment, such as braided hair and the wearing of gold jewelry and fine clothes. Instead, it should be that of your inner self, the unfading beauty of a gentle and quiet spirit, which is of great worth in God's sight. (1 Peter 3:3-4)

CHAPTER THREE

The "it" of Lack of Submission

DEFINITION: Submission is a willingness to yield or surrender to somebody and the act of doing so. Biblical submission is expressed in both attitude and conduct and occurs under leadership that is set in order by God.

FACTS ABOUT SUBMISSION:

Authority comes from God. Romans 13 indicates that all legitimate authority is given by God. God-given authority provides organization and direction in society, government, the church, and the home.

You are to obey authorities. Hebrews 13:17 indicates you are to submit to those over you because they must give an account to God. You are to obey and submit in a way that it will be a joy and not a burden for them.

Rebellion is the opposite of submission. Romans 13 indicates that all legitimate authority is from God, so when you rebel against authority you are actually rebelling against God.

You learn submission by submitting to God. James 4:7 indicates if you submit yourself to God, the devil will flee from you. As you submit to God, it will be easier to submit to others-- your spouse, authority, your employer, etc.

Leaders in the Kingdom of God are to be servants to those who are under authority, not to "lord it over them" (Luke 22:25-26). A biblical attitude exhibited by a leader makes it easy for those under him to submit to his direction.

When the divine order of submission is instituted, relationships are set right, rebellion ceases, and harmony and unity result.

Submission is not abuse. When submission becomes destructive and abusive, it is an affront to true biblical submission. Discipleship--submission as it has also been called--has often been abused in the Church. Discipleship and biblical submission are not the same as when a leader controls every aspect of your life and excludes from the fellowship those who do not conform. Never submit to abuse in any situation. That is not a scriptural concept of submission.

Submission in the home. The wife is to be in submission to the husband, the husband is to be in submission to God (Ephesians 5:22), and the children are to obey their parents (Colossians 3:20). Husbands are told to love their wives as Jesus loved the Church. If a man really loves with the self-sacrificing love with which Christ loved the Church, his wife will desire to please him in all things just as a true believer desires to please Jesus. Christ is perfect in His love for the Church, even though the Church is not perfect in its submission to Him. The husband should demonstrate similar love towards his wife, even if she is not perfect in her submission to him. A wife who is a true believer whose husband loves her in this manner, will seek to please him and submit to his leadership, even as she does to Christ. A man should not force his wife into submission. She is to submit voluntarily because of the Christ-like love shown by her husband. Biblical submission does not mean submission to a godless man. It is describing married life between two Spirit-filled believers who have a natural relationship similar to the spiritual one between Christ and the Church. Paul is saying that if a woman is married to a Christian man who has this type of love for them, then they should be in submission to him (Ephesians 5:22). The husband is to cherish and nourish his wife because they are one flesh and they are both members of Christ's Body. The wife is to be the most important person in the husband's life. He is to leave father, mother, and all others and be joined to his wife. He is to love his wife as he loves his own body. This makes her submission to him a joy. She can submit easily to him, just as she submits to the Lord

We are to submit to one another in the Lord. Believers, both male and female, husband and wife, are to submit to one another, desiring to please each other: *"Submitting yourselves one to another in the fear of God" (Ephesians 5:21).*

Submission does not justify sin. In Acts chapter 5, a woman named Sapphira agreed to her husband's plan to defraud God and the church and she was held personally accountable for her sin. You cannot excuse sin by saying you were forced to do something by someone in authority. If you are asked to do something contrary to God's Word, you must decline. As the disciples who were forbidden to preach the Word, you must obey God rather than man (Acts 4:18-20).

DEALING WITH SUBMISSION:

Pray for any improper submissions to be broken. Do not allow a leader to dictate how you live your life. It is good to accept biblical counsel, but that is different than someone dictating decisions that should be made between you and God alone.   Do not accept abuse from an ungodly mate in the name of "submission". Do not allow abuse of children. Remove yourself and your children from abusive situations.

Pray a prayer of submission. Submit yourself to God first, then ask Him to help you be properly submissive to authorities in your life.

Lead with love and compassion. In your home, on the job, or in the church--if you are in a position of leadership, lead as becomes a true believer, serving with love and compassion.

WHAT GOD'S WORD SAYS ABOUT SUBMISSION:

Jesus said to them, "The kings of the Gentiles lord it over them; and those who exercise authority over them call themselves Benefactors. But you are not to be like that. Instead, the greatest among you should be like the youngest, and the one who rules like the one who serves." (Luke 22:25-26)

Then they called them in again and commanded them not to speak or teach at all in the name of Jesus. But Peter and John replied, "Judge for yourselves whether it is right in God's sight to obey you rather than God. For we cannot help speaking about what we have seen and heard." (Acts 4:18-20)

Be devoted to one another in brotherly love. Honor one another above yourselves. (Romans 12:10)

Everyone must submit himself to the governing authorities, for there is no authority except that which God has established. The authorities that exist have been established by God. Consequently, he who rebels against the authority is rebelling against what God has instituted, and those who do so will bring judgment on themselves. For rulers hold no terror for those who do right, but for those who do wrong. Do you want to be free from fear of the one in authority? Then do what is right and he will commend you. For he is God's servant to do you good. But if you do wrong, be afraid, for he does not bear the sword for nothing. He is God's servant, an agent of wrath to bring punishment on the wrongdoer. Therefore, it is necessary to submit to the authorities, not only because of possible punishment but also because of conscience. (Romans 13:1-5)

You, my brothers, were called to be free. But do not use your freedom to indulge the sinful nature; rather, serve one another in love. The entire law is summed up in a single command: "Love your neighbor as yourself." (Galatians 5:13-14)

Wives, submit to your husbands as to the Lord. For the husband is the head of the wife as Christ is the head of the church, his body, of which he is the Savior. Now as the church submits to Christ, so also wives should submit to their husbands in everything. Husbands, love your wives, just as Christ loved the church and gave himself up for her to make her holy, cleansing her by the washing with water through the word, and to present her to himself as a radiant church, without stain or wrinkle or any other blemish, but holy and blameless. In this same way, husbands ought to love their wives as their own bodies. He who loves his wife loves himself. After all, no one ever hated his own body, but he feeds and cares for it, just as Christ does the church--for we are members of his body. For this reason, a man will leave his father and mother and be united to his wife, and the two will become one flesh. This is a profound mystery — but I am talking about Christ and the church. However, each one of you also must love his wife as he loves himself, and the wife must respect her husband. (Ephesians 5:22-33)

Children, obey your parents in the Lord, for this is right. "Honor your father and mother"-which is the first commandment with a promise--that it may go well with you and that you may enjoy long life on the earth. Fathers, do not exasperate your children; instead, bring them up in the training and instruction of the Lord. Slaves, obey your earthly masters with respect and fear, and with sincerity of heart, just as you would obey Christ. Obey them not only to win their favor when their eye is on you, but like slaves of Christ, doing the will of God from your heart. Serve wholeheartedly, as if you were serving the Lord, not men, because you know that the Lord will reward everyone for whatever good he does, whether he is slave or free. And masters, treat your slaves in the same way. Do not threaten them, since you know that he who is both their Master and yours is in heaven, and there is no favoritism with him. (Ephesians 6:1-9)

Wives, submit to your husbands, as is fitting in the Lord. Husbands, love your wives and do not be harsh with them. Children, obey your parents in everything, for this pleases the Lord. Fathers, do not embitter your children, or they will become discouraged. Slaves, obey your earthly masters in everything; and do it, not only when their eye is on you and to win their favor, but with sincerity of heart and reverence for the Lord. Whatever you do, work at it with all your heart, as working for the Lord, not for men, since you know that you will receive an inheritance from the Lord as a reward. It is the Lord Christ you are serving. (Colossians 3:18-24)

You must teach what is in accord with sound doctrine. Teach the older men to be temperate, worthy of respect, self-controlled, and sound in faith, in love and in endurance. Likewise, teach the older women to be reverent in the way they live, not to be slanderers or addicted to much wine, but to teach what is good. Then they can train the younger women to love their husbands and children, to be self-controlled and pure, to be busy at home, to be kind, and to be subject to their husbands, so that no one will malign the word of God. Similarly, encourage the young men to be self-controlled. In everything set them an example by doing what is good. In your teaching show integrity, seriousness and soundness of speech that cannot be condemned, so that those who oppose you may be ashamed because they have nothing bad to say about us. Teach slaves to be subject to their masters in everything, to try to please them, not to talk back to them, and not to steal from them, but to show that they can be fully trusted, so that in every way they will make the teaching about God our Savior attractive. (Titus 2:1-10)

Obey your leaders and submit to their authority. They keep watch over you as men who must give an account. Obey them so that their work will be a joy, not a burden, for that would be of no advantage to you. (Hebrews 13:17)

What causes fights and quarrels among you? Don't they come from your desires that battle within you? You want something but don't get it. You kill and covet, but you cannot have what you want. You quarrel and fight. You do not have, because you do not ask God. When you ask, you do not receive, because you ask with wrong motives, that you may spend what you get on your pleasures. (James 4:1-3)

Submit yourselves, then, to God. Resist the devil, and he will flee from you. (James 4:7)

Submit yourselves for the Lord's sake to every authority instituted among men: whether to the king, as the supreme authority, or to governors, who are sent by him to punish those who do wrong and to commend those who do right. For it is God's will that by doing good you should silence the ignorant talk of foolish men. Live as free men, but do not use your freedom as a cover-up for evil; live as servants of God. Show proper respect to everyone: Love the brotherhood of believers, fear God, honor the king. Slaves, submit yourselves to your masters with all respect, not only to those who are good and considerate, but also to those who are harsh. For it is commendable if a man bears up under the pain of unjust suffering because he is conscious of God. (1 Peter 2:13-19)

Wives, in the same way be submissive to your husbands so that, if any of them do not believe the word, they may be won over without words by the behavior of their wives, when they see the purity and reverence of your lives. Your beauty should not come from outward adornment, such as braided hair and the wearing of gold jewelry and fine clothes. Instead, it should be that of your inner self, the unfading beauty of a gentle and quiet spirit, which is of great worth in God's sight. For this is the way the holy women of the past who put their hope in God used to make themselves beautiful. They were submissive to their own husbands, like Sarah, who obeyed Abraham and called him her master. You are her daughters if you do what is right and do not give way to fear. Husbands, in the same way be considerate as you live with your wives, and treat them with respect as the weaker partner and as heirs with you of the gracious gift of life, so that nothing will hinder your prayers. Finally, all of you, live in harmony with one another; be sympathetic, love as brothers, be compassionate and humble. Do not repay evil with evil or insult with insult, but with blessing, because to this you were called so that you may inherit a blessing. (1 Peter 3:1-8)

Young men, in the same way be submissive to those who are older. All of you, clothe yourselves with humility toward one another, because, "God opposes the proud but gives grace to the humble." Therefore, humble yourselves under the mighty hand of God, that He may exalt you in due time. (1 Peter 5:5-6)

CHAPTER FOUR

**The "it" of Abuse
(Domestic, Child, Sexual)**

DEFINITION: Abuse is mistreatment of another person. It includes child abuse, spousal abuse, physical, emotional, mental, and sexual abuse. The term also applies to the misuse of legitimate authority, for example a government official or religious leader who abuses their power.

FACTS ABOUT ABUSE:

Abuse takes many forms. It may be domestic abuse, child abuse, sexual abuse, or physical, emotional, and mental abuse.

Abuse is not tolerated in God's Kingdom. Certain types of abuse--such as domestic abuse--is permitted in some countries, but we are not citizens of the nation in which we live. We are citizens of the Kingdom of God, and we are governed by God's laws that prohibit any kind of abuse.

Abuse is against the law in the US and many other nations. See God's mandates regarding believers abiding by the law in Romans 13:1-3; 1 Peter 2:13-14; and Luke 17:2.

Abuse is against God's law. One of the two greatest commandments is to love others (Matthew 22:37-39). Abuse is not love.

Abuse can be learned behavior--for example, a person sees their Dad abuse their Mom and models similar abuse in their own relationships.

Causes of abuse. The root cause behind abuse is often uncontrolled anger. It also stems from a low self-image which makes a person abuse other to try to elevate their own status.

Abusers tend to justify their behavior. They blame others for making them so angry that they are forced to respond in this manner.

DEALING WITH ABUSE:

If you are being abused, remove yourself from the situation. Remaining in an abusive situation may cost your life or that of your child. In many nations, you are legally responsible for removing a child from an abusive environment. Move in with a relative or friend or seek help from a Christian shelter. If you are being abused by an employer, seek a new job. If you are experiencing abuse by a spiritual leader, find a new church.

If you are the abuser, admit your problem. As long as you are in denial, you cannot change.

Ask God for forgiveness if you have abused someone. Abuse in any form is a sin and violates God's law of loving others (Matthew 22:37-39).

Ask forgiveness of those you have abused. God requires it. Your own gifts, prayers, and worship won't be accepted until you do this: *"Therefore, if you are offering your gift at the altar and there remember that your brother has something against you, leave your gift there in front of the altar. First go and be reconciled to your brother; then come and offer your gift" (Matthew 5:23-24).*

If you tend to be abusive, ask God to develop the Fruit of the Spirit in your life. Love, patience, and self-control will replace your abusive behavior.

If you have suffered abuse, the first step towards healing is to acknowledge that the abuse happened. Maybe your abuser warned you not to tell anyone, or maybe your family didn't believe you when you told them what happened. Healing starts when you admit the truth about the abuse, whether or not others believe you. As you admit the abuse, you may experience feelings of confusion, hurt, blame, and shame. You might be tempted to drown those feelings with alcohol, drugs, food, anger or sexual addictions. Instead, replace these negative thoughts with the truth of God's Word. God made you in His image (Genesis 1:27). He loves you so much that He sent His Only Son to die for you (John 3:16). He has a plan to give you a future and a hope. Admit that what was done to you was wrong, sinful acts committed by sinful people, Whether or not you are able to confront your abuser, you must forgive them. When anger or shameful thoughts over past abuse try to return to your mind, reject these immediately. You will never have a future as long as you are living in the past.

WHAT GOD'S WORD SAYS ABOUT ABUSE:

Abuse in general.

Jesus replied: "'Love the Lord your God with all your heart and with all your soul and with all your mind.' This is the first and greatest commandment. And the second is like it: 'Love your neighbor as yourself.'"   (Matthew 22:37-39)

But the fruit of the Spirit is love, joy, peace, patience, kindness, goodness, faithfulness, gentleness and self-control. (Galatians 5:22-23a)

Sexual abuse.

No one is to approach any close relative to have sexual relations. (Leviticus 18:6)

Do not have sexual relations with your son's daughter or your daughter's daughter; that would dishonor you. (Leviticus 18:10)

Do you not know that the wicked will not inherit the kingdom of God? Do not be deceived: Neither the sexually immoral nor idolaters nor adulterers nor male prostitutes nor homosexual offenders nor thieves nor the greedy nor drunkards nor slanderers nor swindlers will inherit the kingdom of God. And that is what some of you were. But you were washed, you were sanctified, you were justified in the name of the Lord Jesus Christ and by the Spirit of our God. (1 Corinthians 6:9-11)

Child abuse.

See that you do not look down on one of these little ones. For I tell you that their angels in heaven always see the face of my Father in heaven. (Matthew 18:10)

Things that cause people to sin are bound to come, but woe to that person through whom they come. It would be better for him to be thrown into the sea with a millstone tied around his neck than for him to cause one of these little ones to sin. (Luke 17:1-2)

Fathers, do not exasperate your children; instead, bring them up in the training and instruction of the Lord. (Ephesians 6:4)

Spousal Abuse.

Husbands, love your wives, just as Christ loved the church and gave himself up for her to make her holy, cleansing her by the washing with water through the word, and to present her to himself as a radiant church, without stain or wrinkle or any other blemish, but holy and blameless. In this same way, husbands ought to love their wives as their own bodies. He who loves his wife loves himself. After all, no one ever hated his own body, but he feeds and cares for it, just as Christ does the church--for we are members of his body. For this reason, a man will leave his father and mother and be united to his wife, and the two will become one flesh. This is a profound mystery--but I am talking about Christ and the church. However, each one of you also must love his wife as he loves himself, and the wife must respect her husband. (Ephesians 5:25-32)

Wives, submit to your husbands, as is fitting in the Lord. Husbands, love your wives and do not be harsh with them. Children, obey your parents in everything, for this pleases the Lord. (Colossians 3:18-20)

CHAPTER FIVE

The "it" of Adultery

DEFINITION: Adultery is sexual intercourse with someone other than your lawful spouse. It is sin and a flagrant violation of the covenant of marriage.

FACTS ABOUT ADULTERY:

Adultery has many negative consequences. Broken homes, unwanted pregnancies, sexually transmitted diseases, and negative emotions like guilt, fear, shame, and anxiety.

Adultery is sin. According to the Bible, adultery is sin and stems from your own selfish desires. It is not a "weakness". It is not an "affair". It is sin, because God says it is sin. The very thought of it by lusting is sin (Matthew 5:27-28).

God's plan is one man and one woman for life. *"Haven't you read," he replied, "that at the beginning the Creator 'made them male and female,' and said, 'For this reason a man will leave his father and mother and be united to his wife, and the two will become one flesh'? So, they are no longer two, but one. Therefore, what God has joined together, let man not separate"* (Matthew 19:4-6).

DEALING WITH ADULTERY:

Reject lustful thoughts. Lusting after someone is considered the same as adultery (Matthew 5:27-28). Adultery begins in the mind.

Avoid temptation. Avoid compromising situations that put you in a place of temptation, alone with a handsome man or a beautiful woman. If you are never alone with someone of the opposite sex who is not your spouse, adultery will probably not become an issue.

Confess adultery as sin. *"He who conceals his sins does not prosper, but whoever confesses and renounces them finds mercy"* (Proverbs 28:13).

Break ungodly relationships. Break the relationship with your adulterous partner. Make a total break: No more communication in any form. *"Therefore, come out from them and be separate, says the Lord. Touch no unclean thing, and I will receive you. I will be a Father to you, and you will be my sons and daughters, says the Lord Almighty"* (2 Corinthians 6:17-18).

Seek forgiveness from those you have wronged. This would include your spouse and your adulterous partner.

Ask God to restore your marriage. If both parties are willing--with the help of God--your marriage can be restored. If you are the offender, you must realize that your spouse may opt not to take you back. You must be prepared to face this possibility and graciously accept it if it happens.

WHAT GOD'S WORD SAYS ABOUT ADULTERY:

Do not have sexual relations with your neighbor's wife and defile yourself with her. (Leviticus 18:20)

You shall not commit adultery. (Deuteronomy 5:18)

The eye of the adulterer watches for dusk; he thinks, "No eye will see me," and he keeps his face concealed. (Job 24:15)

The lips of an adulteress drip honey, and her speech is smoother than oil; but in the end, she is bitter gall, sharp as a double-edged sword. Her feet go down to death; her steps lead straight to the grave. (Proverbs 5:3 and 5)

Keep to a path far from her, do not go near the door of her house, lest you give your best strength to others and your years to one who is cruel, lest strangers feast on your wealth and your toil enrich another man's house. (Proverbs 5:8-10)

Why be captivated, my son, by an adulteress? Why embrace the bosom of another man's wife? For a man's ways are in full view of the Lord, and he examines all his paths. The evil deeds of a wicked man ensnare him; the cords of his sin hold him fast. (Proverbs 5:20-22)

Can a man scoop fire into his lap without his clothes being burned? Can a man walk on hot coals without his feet being scorched? So is he who sleeps with another man's wife; no one who touches her will go unpunished...A man who commits adultery lacks judgment; whoever does so destroy himself. (Proverbs 6:27-29 and 32)

Say to wisdom, "You are my sister," and call understanding your kinsman; they will keep you from the adulteress, from the wayward wife with her seductive words. (Proverbs 7:4-5)

The mouth of an adulteress is a deep pit; he who is under the Lord's wrath will fall into it. (Proverbs 22:14)

This is the way of an adulteress: She eats and wipes her mouth and says, "I've done nothing wrong." (Proverbs 30:20)

I supplied all their needs, yet they committed adultery and thronged to the houses of prostitutes. (Jeremiah 5:7)

"You have heard that it was said, 'Do not commit adultery.' But I tell you that anyone who looks at a woman lustfully has already committed adultery with her in his heart." (Mathew 5:27-28)

"Haven't you read," he replied, "that at the beginning the Creator made them male and female, and said, 'For this reason a man will leave his father and mother and be united to his wife, and the two will become one flesh'? So, they are no longer two, but one. Therefore, what God has joined together, let man not separate." (Matthew 19:4-6)

Do you not know that the wicked will not inherit the kingdom of God? Do not be deceived: Neither the sexually immoral nor idolaters nor adulterers nor male prostitutes nor homosexual offenders nor thieves nor the greedy nor drunkards nor slanderers nor swindlers will inherit the kingdom of God. And that is what some of you were. But you were washed, you were sanctified, you were justified in the name of the Lord Jesus Christ and by the Spirit of our God. (1 Corinthians 6:9-11)

Flee from sexual immorality. All other sins a man commits are outside his body, but he who sins sexually sins against his own body. Do you not know that your body is a temple of the Holy Spirit, who is in you, whom you have received from God? You are not your own; you were bought at a price. Therefore, honor God with your body. (1 Corinthians 6:18-20)

Marriage should be honored by all, and the marriage bed kept pure, for God will judge the adulterer and all the sexually immoral. (Hebrews 13:4)

With eyes full of adultery, they never stop sinning; they seduce the unstable; they are experts in greed an accursed brood! (2 Peter 2:14)

CHAPTER SIX

The "it" of Unfaithfulness

DEFINITION: Unfaithfulness means to be untrue to a duty, obligation, or promise. It means being untrustworthy or acting as a traitor. The Bible speaks of several types of unfaithfulness: Unfaithfulness to God and His work, to friends and family, and to a spouse.

FACTS ABOUT UNFAITHFULNESS:

Unfaithfulness to God. When you accept Jesus as Savior, you are promising to make Him the Lord of your life. When you violate your promise, and do things your own way or turn your back on God or His Word, you are being unfaithful.   Without faith, it is impossible to please Him (Hebrews 11:6). The parable of the talents in Matthew 5 confirms the importance of faithfulness.

An unfaithful spouse. Unfaithfulness to a mate--adultery--is biblical grounds for divorce (Matthew 19:9), but you are not required to divorce an unfaithful mate. The alternative is to seek to restore the relationship if both parties are willing. The erring party must be forgiven, both by God and their spouse. The unfaithful person must be absolutely discreet and honest about any dealings with the opposite sex in the future in order to rebuild trust.

An unfaithful friend.   An unfaithful friend can be a source of great disappointment. Perhaps they reject you or expose your confidences.   The Bible says *"Like a bad tooth or a lame foot is reliance on the unfaithful in times of trouble" (Proverbs 25:29).*

DEALING WITH UNFAITHFULNESS:

Acknowledge unfaithfulness as sin. Whatever is not of faith is sin (Romans 14:23). Acts of unfaithfulness, unbelief, iniquity, etc.--anything that is not of faith is sin and must be acknowledged as such.

Confess your unfaithfulness to God. Confess and ask forgiveness: *"If we confess our sins, he is faithful and just and will forgive us our sins and purify us from all unrighteousness. If we claim we have not sinned, we make him out to be a liar and his word has no place in our lives" (1 John 1:9-10).*

Confess unfaithfulness to your spouse and seek forgiveness. Ask forgiveness from your mate, seek reconciliation, and break the adulterous relationship. If reconciliation with your spouse is the goal, then the incident must be forgiven and never again brought up. When Satan tries to bring up the past, these thoughts must be rejected.

Confess unfaithfulness to friends and family. Ask those affected by your unfaithfulness to forgive you.

Forgive an unfaithful friend. Forgive your friend, then go to them according to the pattern described in Matthew 18:15-17. If he rejects you, then let him remain an acquaintance instead of a close friend. If he accepts you, pray together for restoration of the friendship. If a friend is abusive or leads you into sin, addictions, or violence, do not attempt to reconcile.

WHAT GOD'S WORD SAYS ABOUT UNFAITHFULNESS:

A talebearer reveals secrets, but he who is of a faithful spirit conceals a matter. (Proverbs 11:13)

Like a bad tooth or a lame foot is reliance on the unfaithful in times of trouble. (Proverbs 25:29)

Faithful are the wounds of a friend, But the kisses of an enemy are deceitful. (Proverbs 27:6)

"You have heard that it was said, 'Do not commit adultery.' But I tell you that anyone who looks at a woman lustfully has already committed adultery with her in his heart." (Matthew 5:27-28)

If your brother sins against you, go and show him his fault, just between the two of you. If he listens to you, you have won your brother over. But if he will not listen, take one or two others along, so that every matter may be established by the testimony of two or three witnesses. If he refuses to listen to them, tell it to the church; and if he refuses to listen even to the church, treat him as you would a pagan or a tax collector. (Matthew 18:15-17)

He that is faithful in that which is least is faithful also in much: and he that is unjust in the least is unjust also in much. (Luke 16:10, KJV)

...everything that does not come from faith is sin. (Romans 14:23)

Now it is required that those who have been given a trust must prove faithful. (1 Corinthians 4:2)

Do you not know that the wicked will not inherit the kingdom of God? Do not be deceived: Neither the sexually immoral nor idolaters nor adulterers nor male prostitutes nor homosexual offenders nor thieves nor the greedy nor drunkards nor slanderers nor swindlers will inherit the kingdom of God. And that is what some of you were. But you were washed, you were sanctified, you were justified in the name of the Lord Jesus Christ and by the Spirit of our God. (1 Corinthians 6:9-11)

And the things that thou hast heard of me among many witnesses, the same commit thou to faithful men, who shall be able to teach others also. (2 Timothy 2:2, KJV)

Let us hold fast the profession of our faith without wavering; (for he is faithful that promised;) (Hebrews 10:23, KJV)

And without faith it is impossible to please God, because anyone who comes to him must believe that he exists and that he rewards those who earnestly seek him. (Hebrews 11:6)

If we confess our sins, he is faithful and just and will forgive us our sins and purify us from all unrighteousness. If we claim we have not sinned, we make him out to be a liar and his word has no place in our lives. (1 John 1:9-10)

Do not be afraid of what you are about to suffer. I tell you, the devil will put some of you in prison to test you, and you will suffer persecution for ten days. Be faithful, even to the point of death, and I will give you the crown of life.   (Revelation 2:10)

Read the parable of the faithful servant in Matthew chapter 25.

CHAPTER SEVEN

The "it" of Trust Issues

DEFINITION: Trust is believing in the integrity of someone, that they are who they say they are and will do what they said they will do. It is believing with confident expectation. Biblically, trust is a firm reliance, assurance, and belief on God and His Word. When someone has "trust issues", it means they lack trust in a person, a relationship, or God.

FACTS ABOUT TRUST:

Trust can be misplaced. When dealing with others, your trust can be misplaced and you can be disappointed. This can result in what is termed "trust issues", where you have difficulty trusting someone because of disappointments in the past.

Trust in God is never misplaced. The Psalmist said: *"Some trust in chariots and some in horses, but we trust in the name of the Lord our God" (Psalm 20:7).*

Trust is actually an expression of your faith in God. By trusting God, you are showing that you have assurance that He is who He says He is and that His Word is true. Trust also provides assurance of your salvation and eternal destiny.

DEALING WITH TRUST:

Ask God to heal your trust issues. If you have difficulty trusting God or others because of past experiences, ask the Lord to heal these emotions.

Ask forgiveness if you have been untrustworthy. Ask God to forgive you and ask the person you failed to forgive you.

Do not rely on man. This is not to say you should not trust people, but your main trust should be in the Lord. Do not place your trust in untrustworthy people (Proverbs 25:19).

Place your trust in God. Rely on the Lord because He will never fail you (Romans 10:11).

WHAT GOD'S WORD SAYS ABOUT TRUST:

The Lord himself goes before you and will be with you; he will never leave you nor forsake you. Do not be afraid; do not be discouraged. (Deuteronomy 31:8)

And those who know Your name will put their trust in You; For You, Lord, have not forsaken those who seek You. (Psalm 9:10, NKJV)

Help, Lord for the godly are no more; the faithful have vanished from among men. (Psalms 12:1)

Some trust in chariots and some in horses., but we trust in the name of the Lord our God. (Psalm 20:7)

For the king trusts in the Lord; through the unfailing love of the Most High he will not be shaken. (Psalm 21:7)

To you, 0 Lord, I lift up my soul; in you I trust, 0 my God. O my God, I trust in You; Let me not be ashamed; Let not my enemies triumph over me. (Psalm 25:1-2)

In You, O Lord, I put my trust; Let me never be ashamed; Deliver me in Your righteousness. (Psalm 31:1, NKJV)

 I trust in you, O Lord; I say, "You are my God." (Psalm 31:14)

Many are the woes of the wicked, but the Lord's unfailing love surrounds the man who trusts in him. (Psalm 32:10)

In him our hearts rejoice, for we trust in his holy name. (Psalm 33:21)

Trust in the Lord and do good. (Psalm 37:3)

Blessed is the man who makes the Lord his trust. (Psalm 40:4)

I am like an olive tree flourishing in the house of God; I trust in God's unfailing love forever and ever. (Psalm 52:8)

But as for me, I trust in you. (Psalm 55:23)

When I am afraid, I will trust in you. In God, whose word I praise, in God I trust; I will not be afraid. What can mortal man do to me? (Psalm 56:3-4)

Trust in him at all times, 0 people; pour out your hearts to him, for God is our refuge. (Psalm 62:8)

You are my God; save your servant who trusts in you. (Psalm 86:2)

I will say of the Lord, "He is my refuge and my fortress; My God, in Him I will trust." (Psalm 91:2)

It is better to take refuge in the Lord than to trust in man. It is better to take refuge in the Lord than to trust in princes. (Psalm 118:8-9)

Those who trust in the Lord are like Mount Zion, which cannot be shaken but endures forever. (Psalm 125:1)

Let the morning bring me word of your unfailing love, for I have put my trust in you. (Psalm 143:8)

Do not put your trust in princes, nor in a son of man, in whom there is no help. (Psalm 146:3, NKJV)

Trust in the Lord with all your heart and lean not on your own understanding; in all your ways acknowledge him and, he will make your paths straight. (Proverbs 3:5-6)

Like a bad tooth or a lame foot is reliance on the unfaithful in times of trouble. (Proverbs 25:19)

Fear of man will prove to be a snare, but whoever trusts in the Lord is kept safe. (Proverbs 29:25)

Trust in the Lord forever, for the Lord, the Lord, is the Rock eternal. (Isaiah 26:4)

Let him who walks in the dark, who has no light, trust in the name of the Lord and rely on his God. (Isaiah 50:10)

This is what the Lord says: "Cursed is the one who trusts in man, who depends on flesh for his strength and whose heart turns away from the Lord." (Jeremiah 17:5)

Blessed is the man who trusts in the Lord, whose confidence is in him. (Jeremiah 17:7)

Whoever can be trusted with very little can also be trusted with much, and whoever is dishonest with very little will also be dishonest with much. So, if you have not been trustworthy in handling worldly wealth, who will trust you with true riches? And if you have not been trustworthy with someone else's property, who will give you property of your own? (Luke 16:10-12)

Anyone who trusts in him *(God)* will never be put to shame. (Romans 10:11)

I know whom I have believed, and am convinced that he is able to guard what I have entrusted to him for that day. (2 Timothy 1:12)

If we are faithless, he will remain faithful, for he cannot disown himself. (2 Timothy 2:13)

Do not let your hearts be troubled. Trust in God; trust also in me. (John 14:1)

CHAPTER EIGHT

The "it" of Divorce and Remarriage

DEFINITIONS: Divorce occurs when a couple decides they no longer want to fulfill their commitment to their marriage. Remarriage is marrying again after a previous marriage ended in either death or divorce.

FACTS ABOUT DIVORCE AND REMARRIAGE:

Divorce was not God's original plan. When questioned by the religious leaders about divorce, Jesus explained that divorce was permitted because of the hardness of the hearts of mankind (Mark 10:1-9). God's original plan was one man, one wife, for life (1 Corinthians 7:10)

Divorce is permitted under certain circumstances. For believers, these circumstances include sexual immorality (Matthew 19:9) and when a spouse deserts (1 Corinthians 7:15). In these situations, divorce is permitted by scripture, but not necessarily advocated. The goal is always reconciliation if possible.

Remarriage is not prohibited for a person whose spouse has committed sexual immorality or abandoned them--and of course, remarriage is permitted after the death of a spouse.

Although usually one-person initiates divorce proceedings, both parties most likely have contributed to the breakup to some degree.

Divorce is not the unpardonable sin. We are all sinners, and we all make mistakes in relationships. To those who were caught in sin, Jesus forgave them with the admonishment, "go your way and sin no more." Sinful errors may have been made in a relationship, but you can receive forgiveness and go on with a renewed dedication to God.

Having an unbelieving spouse is not grounds for divorce. The Christian spouse is encouraged to remain with their mate with the goal of winning him/her to Christ (1 Corinthians 7:12-16).

Many problems in marriage would be avoided if believers obeyed God's Word regarding not marrying an unbeliever (2 Corinthians 6:14-18). No need to pray about this. God already said don't do it! To avoid such emotional entanglements, don't date unbelievers.

DEALING WITH DIVORCE AND REMARRIAGE:

Think long and hard before initiating a divorce. Do you have biblical grounds? How will it affect your children, friends, and family? Will it actually solve problems or just present a whole set of new issues? How will it affect you and your family financially? Divorces are difficult spiritually, mentally, materially, and a breakup is especially hard on the children. Shame, anger, depression, loss of other relationships--all are part of divorce. You shouldn't leave because of petty issues of incompatibility, because you tire of a relationship, or you are not committed enough to make it through the tough times.

Explore your relationship with God. Are you a believer? If you want your marriage to succeed, you must build it on the Lord (Psalm 127:1). Join with your spouse to seek a renewed relationship with God first, then with each other.

Seek forgiveness. Ask forgiveness from God and from your spouse. Pray for the healing of your emotions and relationship.

Seek reconciliation. Try to the best of your ability to reconcile with your spouse. Pray together, study the Word of God, form relationships with couples who have successful marriages, attend Christian marriage seminars. Pray about your problems instead of yelling about them. Do not bring up the past. Look to the future.

Take practical actions. List all the praiseworthy traits of your spouse and share at least one each day with them. Take a good look at yourself and improve things like bad habits, appearance, mannerisms, integrity, etc. Don't just tell your spouse how you are going to change; show him/her by changing.

If you are a born-again believer, do not marry an unsaved person. Don't be surprised when such a union experiences difficulty because Jesus said, a house divided against itself is destined to fall (Luke 11:17). A similar passage in the Amplified Version says, *"...no city or house divided against itself will last or continue to stand" (Matthew 12:25 AMP).*

Accept that sometimes, there is no more you can do. If you have done everything possible to save your marriage and it still failed, if your mate has departed, or if you are in an abusive situation and you need to depart for your own safety--then accept that there is nothing more you can do. It is in God's hands. Divorce is not the unpardonable sin. Ask God for forgiveness for your part in the problem. Accept His forgiveness, forgive yourself, and then get on with your life. Do not keep looking back thinking "I should have...." As long as you live in the past, you will never have a future.

Realize that there are some relationships that cannot be fixed. Not because God can't fix them, but because one party is unwilling to change. The abuser, the alcoholic, the drug addict-- they all promise they won't do it again, but they will not change without a true born-again experience and supernatural deliverance. The adulterer and fornicator that comes and goes in and out of your marriage bed may leave you with an incurable sexually transmitted disease. Perhaps this is one reason why fornication--sexual activity outside of marriage including adultery--was specifically mentioned as a scriptural cause for divorce (Matthew 5:32). In the case of spousal abuse or child abuse, you must leave and take the kids with you. In many nations, you are legally responsible and can be criminally prosecuted if you fail to protect your children. Just because you walk away, does not mean God will not continue to deal with your spouse, nor does it mean God cannot put the relationship back together again in the future, nor does it mean that you must legally divorce your mate. What it means is that, for the present, you must take this action to protect yourself and your children. Be sure to protect yourself legally from the debts of your spouse and be sure the children are provided for.

Know that God is the God of a second chance. Consider Jonah, David, Moses, and Peter. God accomplished His purposes in the lives of each of these men, despite their failures. If you have failed in marriage and you are divorced, it is time to.."*Arise [from the depression and prostration in which circumstances have kept you--rise to a new life]! Shine (be radiant with the glory of the Lord), for your light has come, and the glory of the Lord has risen upon you!" (Isaiah 60:1, TAB)*. Let go of the hurt and bitterness. Stop dwelling on the "what ifs". Stop rehearsing the past. If you are in an abusive situation, stop trying to make it work. If your mate has abandoned you, release them to God. If God puts the relationship back together in the future, then it will work. If not, consider it a divine division, abandon the past, and look to the future. As long as you are living in the past, you will never have a future.

Embrace your loss as spiritual gain. The Apostle Paul said: *"But whatever was to my profit I now consider loss for the sake of Christ. What is more, I consider everything a loss compared to the surpassing greatness of knowing Christ Jesus my Lord, for whose sake I have lost all things. I consider them rubbish, that I may gain Christ and be found in him, not having a righteousness of my own that comes from the law, but that which is through faith in Christ--the righteousness that comes from God and is by faith. I want to know Christ and the power of his resurrection and the fellowship of sharing in his sufferings, becoming like him in his death" (Philippians 3:7-10, KJV)*. God can use even the suffering of divorce to deepen your relationship with Him. Embrace that loss--and all the losses in your life--as spiritual gain.

Do not judge others who have divorced and remarried. If you don't believe in divorce for any reason or remarriage after a divorce, do not judge others who remarry. Live by your own convictions in this area, but do not impose your beliefs on those whose situations you do not understand and know nothing about.

WHAT GOD'S WORD SAYS ABOUT DIVORCE AND REMARRIAGE:

But for Adam no suitable helper was found. So the Lord God caused the man to fall into a deep sleep; and while he was sleeping, he took one of the man's ribs and closed up the place with flesh. Then the Lord God made a woman from the rib he had taken out of the man, and he brought her to the man. The man said, "This is now bone of my bones and flesh of my flesh; she shall be called 'woman,' for she was taken out of man." For this reason, a man will leave his father and mother and be united to his wife, and they will become one flesh. (Genesis 2:20-24)

He who finds a wife finds a good thing, And obtains favor from the Lord. (Proverbs 18:22)

Like a bird that strays from its nest is a man who strays from his home. (Proverbs 27:8)

If a man divorces his wife and she leaves him and marries another man, should he return to her again? Would not the land be completely defiled? (Jeremiah 3:1)

"For I know the plans I have for you," declares the Lord, "plans to prosper you and not to harm you, plans to give you hope and a future." (Jeremiah 29:11)

Can two walk together, except they be agreed? (Amos 3:3)

And did not God make [you and your wife] one [flesh]? Did not one make you and preserve your spirit alive? And why [did God make you two] one? Because He sought a godly offspring [from your union]. Therefore, take heed to yourselves, and let no one deal treacherously and be faithless to the wife of his youth. (Malachi 2:15 AMP)

It has been said, "Anyone who divorces his wife must give her a certificate of divorce." But I tell you that anyone who divorces his wife, except for marital unfaithfulness, causes her to become an adulteress, and anyone who marries the divorced woman commits adultery. (Matthew 5:31-32)

Jesus knew their thoughts and said to them, "Every kingdom divided against itself will be ruined, and every city or household divided against itself will not stand." (Matthew 12:25)

Some Pharisees came to him to test him. They asked, "Is it lawful for a man to divorce his wife for any and every reason?" "Haven't you read," he replied, "that at the beginning the Creator 'made them male and female,'   and said, 'For this reason a man will leave his father and mother and be united to his wife, and the two will become one flesh'? So, they are no longer two, but one. Therefore, what God has joined together, let man not separate."   "Why then," they asked, "did Moses command that a man give his wife a certificate of divorce and send her away?" Jesus replied, "Moses permitted you to divorce your wives because your hearts were hard. But it was not this way from the beginning. I tell you that anyone who divorces his wife, except for marital unfaithfulness, and marries another woman commits adultery."   (Matthew 19:3-9)

Some Pharisees came and tested him by asking, "Is it lawful for a man to divorce his wife?" "What did Moses command you?" he replied. They said, "Moses permitted a man to write a certificate of divorce and send her away." "It was because your hearts were hard that Moses wrote you this law," Jesus replied. "But at the beginning of creation God 'made them male and female.' 'For this reason, a man will leave his father and mother and be united to his wife, and the two will become one flesh.' So, they are no longer two, but one. Therefore, what God has joined together, let man not separate." When they were in the house again, the disciples asked Jesus about this. He answered, "Anyone who divorces his wife and marries another woman commits adultery against her. And if she divorces her husband and marries another man, she commits adultery." (Mark 10:1-9-12)

Anyone who divorces his wife and marries another woman commits adultery, and the man who marries a divorced woman commits adultery. (Luke 16:18)

For example, by law a married woman is bound to her husband as long as he is alive, but if her husband dies, she is released from the law of marriage. So then, if she marries another man while her husband is still alive, she is called an adulteress. But if her husband dies, she is released from that law and is not an adulteress, even though she marries another man. (Romans 7:2-3)

To the married I give this command (not I but the Lord): A wife must not separate from her husband. But if she does, she must remain unmarried or else be reconciled to her husband. And a husband must not divorce his wife. If any brother has a wife who is not a believer and she is willing to live with him, he must not divorce her. And if a woman has a husband who is not a believer and he is willing to live with her, she must not divorce him. But if the unbeliever leaves, let him do so. A believing man or woman is not bound in such circumstances; God has called us to live in peace. (I Corinthians 7:10-15)

A woman is bound to her husband as long as he lives. But if her husband dies, she is free to marry anyone she wishes, but he must belong to the Lord (1 Corinthians 7:39)

Read 1 Corinthians 13.

Do not be yoked together with unbelievers. For what do righteousness and wickedness have in common? Or what fellowship can light have with darkness? What harmony is there between Christ and Belial? What does a believer have in common with an unbeliever? What agreement is there between the temple of God and idols? For we are the temple of the living God. As God has said: "I will live with them and walk among them, and I will be their God, and they will be my people. Therefore come out from them and be separate," says the Lord. "Touch no unclean thing, and I will receive you. I will be a Father to you, and you will be my sons and daughters, says the Lord Almighty." (2 Corinthians 6:14-18, NIV)

Marriage should be honored by all, and the marriage bed kept pure, for God will judge the adulterer and all the sexually immoral. (Hebrews 13:4)

Husbands, in the same way be considerate as you live with your wives, and treat them with respect as the weaker partner and as heirs with you of the gracious gift of life, so that nothing will hinder your prayers. (1 Peter 3:7)

CHAPTER NINE

The "it" of Polygamy

DEFINITION: Polygamy is having multiple spouses at the same time. While this is forbidden by law in many nations, it is still practiced in some cultures.

FACTS ABOUT POLYGAMY:

God's plan is one man, one woman for life. God created a wife for Adam and His plan was that the two become one (Matthew 19:4-6). Divorce was not in God's original plan, but was permitted later because of the "hardness of man's heart" (Matthew 19:8). Polygamy was permitted in Old Testament times, but was not God's original plan.

The first polygamous marriage was Lamech, who took two wives (Genesis 4:19).

Polygamous relationships, although common in the Old Testament, were not successful. For an example, study the family of the Old Testament patriarch Jacob. There was constant friction between his two wives, Leah and Rachel, and their children. Abraham did not officially marry his wife's hand-maiden, Hagar, but he had sexual relationships with her and it resulted in trouble between her and Sarah and their children. The wives of Solomon caused great difficulties and eventually turned his heart away from God (1 Kings 11:3-4). Polygamous relationships in the Old Testament demonstrate the wisdom of God's original plan for one man to have one wife for life.

Polygamy is adultery on a permanent basis. The New Testament says that marriage to another partner while the first partner is still living is adultery (Romans 7:1-3).

A polygamous person should not be a leader in the church. First Timothy 3:2 requires that an elder in a congregation be the husband of only one wife. This does not mean that if a former wife has died or he has a biblically justified divorce he cannot serve. It means that he should not have any polygamous unions.

Polygamy is sin. No one who continues in sexual sins will inherit the Kingdom of God (1 Corinthians 6:9-10).

Sexual sin can be forgiven. As in the case of all sin of which you confess and repent, God will forgive sexual sin. First Corinthians 6:9-10 lists many types of sins, including fornicators and adulterers. Then 1 Corinthians 6: 11 declares: *"And that is what some of you were. But you were washed, you were sanctified, you were justified in the name of the Lord Jesus Christ and by the Spirit of our God."* These believers repented of their sexual sins and were forgiven.

Who is the true mate? In a culture where a man is married to multiple wives, the first wife is the rightful mate if she desires to remain. Since the husband has actually committed adultery by taking additional wives, she has a right to leave according to God's Word. If she chooses to remain, the other wives must be dealt with in an honorable way. The husband should provide financially for them and children of their union.

DEALING WITH POLYGAMY:

Repent of polygamy. As with any other sin, confession and repentance is required.

Change your lifestyle. A man with multiple wives should remain with his first wife--if she agrees--while continuing to provide for his other wives and children financially. Sexual relationships with all other wives should cease.

Cease any involvement with polygamy. This would include religions that foster it, people that practice it, and Internet websites, literature, or media that promote it.

WHAT GOD'S WORD SAYS ABOUT POLYGAMY:

Then the Lord God made a woman from the rib he had taken out of the man, and he brought her to the man. The man said, "This is now bone of my bones and flesh of my flesh; she shall be called 'woman,' for she was taken out of man." For this reason, a man will leave his father and mother and be united to his wife, and they will become one flesh. (Genesis 2:22-24)

He must not take many wives, or his heart will be led astray. (Deuteronomy 17:17)

"Haven't you read," he replied, "that at the beginning the Creator 'made them male and female,' and said, 'For this reason a man will leave his father and mother and be united to his wife, and the two will become one flesh'? So, they are no longer two, but one. Therefore, what God has joined together, let man not separate." (Matthew 19:4-6)

I tell you that anyone who divorces his wife, except for marital unfaithfulness, and marries another woman commits adultery. (Matthew 19:9)

...by law a married woman is bound to her husband as long as he is alive, but if her husband dies, she is released from the law of marriage. So then, if she marries another man while her husband is still alive, she is called an adulteress. But if her husband dies, she is released from that law and is not an adulteress, even though she marries another man. (Romans 7:2-3)

Do you not know that the wicked will not inherit the kingdom of God? Do not be deceived: Neither the sexually immoral nor idolaters nor adulterers nor male prostitutes nor homosexual offenders nor thieves nor the greedy nor drunkards nor slanderers nor swindlers will inherit the kingdom of God. And that is what some of you were. But you were washed, you were sanctified, you were justified in the name of the Lord Jesus Christ and by the Spirit of our God. (1 Corinthians 6:9-11)

Nevertheless, because of sexual immorality, let each man have his own wife, and let each woman have her own husband. (1 Corinthians 7:2)

Now the overseer must be above reproach, the husband of but one wife, temperate, self-controlled, respectable, hospitable, able to teach, not given to drunkenness, not violent but gentle, not quarrelsome, not a lover of money. (1 Timothy 3:2-3)

CHAPTER TEN

The "it" of Incest

DEFINITION: Incest is sexual relations between close relatives.

FACTS ABOUT INCEST:

Incest is against the law in many nations. It is punishable by imprisonment and, in some societies, by death.

Incest is sin. Whether or not incest is considered illegal by the society in which you live or whether or not it is consensual, it is sin in God's sight. Leviticus 18:6-18 is very clear about this.

Incest is abuse. Incest is abusive, with one person exercising sexual power over another. Such abuse results in many other problems. For example, sexually abused children often suffer from low self-image, are depressed, and harbor thoughts of suicide. Many run away from the abusive situation and get involved in addictions and other deviant sexual behaviors such as prostitution and homosexuality.

Incest can result in genetic disorders. Congenital disorders, birth defects, disabilities, and death are caused by inbreeding.

DEALING WITH INCEST:

If you are committing incest--stop it immediately. Admit it as sin and seek forgiveness from God and from the person against whom or with whom you committed this sin. As with all sin, forgiveness is available through Jesus Christ.

If you are presently a victim of incest--tell someone. Tell a trusted friend who can help you escape and/or confront the abuser. If you are underage, tell authorities who have the power to remove you from the situation. Do not be intimidated by family members who do not believe you or do not want you to reveal the truth.

If have been a victim of incest--forgive your abuser and ask God to heal you from the mental, emotional, and physical effects of the abuse. God has promised to heal the brokenhearted (Psalm 147:3). If you were a victim, the incest was not your fault. You were forced to do something degrading and your are not responsible for the wrong that was done to you.

Turn to God's Word and prayer for comfort, healing, and deliverance. Make these practices part of your everyday life. Whether you were a victim of incest or a perpetrator of it, prayer and the Word will heal your pain and change your life.

WHAT GOD'S WORD SAYS ABOUT INCEST:

No one is to approach any close relative to have sexual relations. I am the Lord. Do not dishonor your father by having sexual relations with your mother. She is your mother; do not have relations with her. Do not have sexual relations with your father's wife; that would dishonor your father. Do not have sexual relations with your sister, either your father's daughter or your mother's daughter, whether she was born in the same home or elsewhere. Do not have sexual relations with your son's daughter or your daughter's daughter; that would dishonor you. Do not have sexual relations with the daughter of your father's wife, born to your father; she is your sister. Do not have sexual relations with your father's sister; she is your father's close relative. Do not have sexual relations with your mother's sister, because she is your mother's close relative. Do not dishonor your father's brother by approaching his wife to have sexual relations; she is your aunt. Do not have sexual relations with your daughter-in-law. She is your son's wife; do not have relations with her. Do not have sexual relations with your brother's wife; that would dishonor your brother. Do not have sexual relations with both a woman and her daughter. Do not have sexual relations with either her son's daughter or her daughter's daughter; they are her close relatives. That is wickedness. Do not take your wife's sister as a rival wife and have sexual relations with her while your wife is living. (Leviticus 18:6-18)

If a man marries his sister, the daughter of either his father or his mother, and they have sexual relations, it is a disgrace. They must be cut off before the eyes of their people. He has dishonored his sister and will be held responsible. (Leviticus 20:17)

It is actually reported that there is sexual immorality among you, and of a kind that does not occur even among pagans: A man has his father's wife. And you are proud! Shouldn't you rather have been filled with grief and have put out of your fellowship the man who did this? Even though I am not physically present, I am with you in spirit. And I have already passed judgment on the one who did this, just as if I were present. When you are assembled in the name of our Lord Jesus and I am with you in spirit, and the power of our Lord Jesus is present, hand this man over to Satan, so that the sinful nature may be destroyed and his spirit saved on the day of the Lord. (1 Corinthians 5:1-5)

CHAPTER ELEVEN

The "it" of Communication Issues

DEFINITION: Communication is the act of giving or exchanging information through speech, writing, various forms of media and the arts, or through a common system of signs or behavior.

FACTS ABOUT COMMUNICATION:

The most important communication is that between God and man. God communicates through His Word and the gifts of the Holy Spirit such as prophecy and teaching.

The Holy Spirit communicates to convict us of sin (John 16:7-11) and to guide us into all truth (John 16:13).

Our primary mode of communication with God is prayer. In prayer, we speak with God and He speaks to us.

God has given you the ability to communicate. He has also declared that you will give an account on the day of judgment for every careless word you have spoken (Matthew 12:36).

Your tongue is powerful. The Bible says it has the power of life and death in it (Proverbs 18:21). Your own words can be a snare to your soul (Proverbs 18:7).

Your mouth, speaking God's Word, expedites the work of angels. The angels of God are released or hindered to work in your behalf by the words that come out of your mouth. Hebrews 1:14 reveals that angels are "ministering spirits" sent from God to minister in behalf of the heirs of salvation. They are released by God to minister when you speak God's Word instead of murmuring and complaining (Psalm 103:20).

The tongues is difficult to control. James 3:1-3 explains that the tongue is impossible to tame, apart from the Holy Spirit. The Bible compares the tongue to a fire (James 3:5); a world of iniquity (James 3:6); a beast that needs taming (James 3:7-8); a fountain of either fresh or bitter water (James 3:11); a tree bearing either good or evil fruit (James 3:12); an unruly evil (James 3:8); deadly poison (James 3:8); a sharp razor (Psalms 52:2); a sharp sword (Psalms 57:4; 59:7); a poisonous serpent (Psalms 140:3); and a deep pit (Proverbs 22:14).

What you speak comes out of your heart. If your heart is filled with negative thoughts--hatred, anger, jealousy, pride, bitterness, and strife--that is what will come out of your mouth. If your heart and mind are filled with carnal thoughts and lusts of the flesh, this will be manifested in your words. If your heart and mind are filled with positive thoughts--thoughts of faith, love, joy, peace--what you say will reflect this.

Controlling your tongues is mandatory because:

-You can be snared with your own words: *"You are snared by the words of your mouth;*

You are taken by the words of your mouth" (Proverbs 6:2, NKJV).

-Your words can separate you from God: "*Who have said, with our tongue will we prevail; our lips are our own: who is lord over us?" (Psalms 12:4, KJV).*

-Your words can create a breach--an opening--in your spirit: "*A wholesome tongue is a tree of life: but perverseness therein is a breach in the spirit" (Proverbs 15:4, KJV).*

-Satan uses your lips to affect your soul: "*A fool's mouth is his destruction, and his lips are the snare of his soul" (Proverbs 18:7, KJV).*

-You tongue can cause calamity: "*He who guards his mouth and his tongue keeps himself from calamity" (Proverbs 21:23).*

-Your tongue affects your whole body: "*And the tongue is a fire, a world of iniquity. The tongue is so set among our members that it defiles the whole body, and sets on fire the course of nature; and it is set on fire by hell" (James 3:6, NKJV).*

-Your tongue affects your whole life: "*He who guards his mouth preserves his life, but he who opens wide his lips shall have destruction" (Proverbs 13:3, NKJV).*

DEALING WITH COMMUNICATION:

Ask God to forgive you. Evil communication is sin, and as all sin, must be dealt with by confession, repentance, and seeking forgiveness through Jesus Christ.

Get your heart right with God. The first step in gaining victory over the tongue is to get your heart right with God because..."*the things that come out of the mouth come from the heart, and these make a man 'unclean.' For out of the heart come evil thoughts, murder, adultery, sexual immorality, theft, false testimony, slander" (Matthew 15:18-20).* Your mouth speaks what is in your heart. If your heart is not right, your tongue will reveal it.

Recognize that you are responsible for the words that come out of your mouth, so take control! "*But I tell you that men will have to give account on the day of judgment for every careless word they have spoken. For by your words you will be acquitted, and by your words you will be condemned" (Matthew 12:36-37).*

Keep your words few and simple. The more you talk, the greater the opportunity to sin with your words. "*When words are many, sin is not absent, but he who holds his tongue is wise" (Proverbs 10:19)."* Jesus said: " *Simply let your 'Yes' be 'Yes,' and your 'No,' 'No'; anything beyond this comes from the evil one" (Matthew 5:37).*

Set a good example by your communications. Your conversation reflects on the Lord, so you should set a good example by what you say: "*... set an example for the believers in speech, in life, in love, in faith and in purity" (1Timothy 4:12).*

Think before you speak. Take time to think about what you are going to say. The Bible warns:

Therefore, my beloved brethren, let every man be swift to hear; slow to speak, slow to wrath. (James 1:19, KJV)

If you have played the fool and exalted yourself, or if you have planned evil, clap your hand over your mouth! (Proverbs 30:32)

The heart of the righteous weighs its answers, but the mouth of the wicked gushes evil. (Proverbs 15:28)

Even a fool is thought wise if he keeps silent, and discerning if he holds his tongue. (Proverbs 17:28)

Think on these verses before you speak.

The wise in heart are called prudent, understanding, and knowing, and winsome speech increases learning [in both speaker and listener]. (Proverbs 16:21, AMP)

The mind of the wise instructs his mouth, and adds learning and persuasiveness to his lips. (Proverbs 16:23, AMP)

A man has joy in making an apt answer, and a word spoken at the right moment--how good it is! (Proverbs 15:23, AMP)

A word fitly spoken is like apples of gold in pictures of silver. (Proverbs 25:11, KJV)

He who guards his mouth and his tongue keeps himself from calamity. (Proverbs 21:23)

He who guards his lips guards his life, but he who speaks rashly will come to ruin. (Proverbs 13:3)

Ask yourself these questions before you speak.
-Will what I am about to say bring glory to God?
-Is it the truth?
-Is it fair to all concerned?
-Will it be beneficial to all concerned?
-Will it edify others?
-Have I talked to the person I am talking about?
-Is what I am saying a fact that needs to be shared or is what I am saying based on rumors and does not need to be said?
-Is it absolutely necessary that I share this?

Separate yourself from those who cannot control their tongues.   The Bible warns: *"Stay away from a foolish man, for you will not find knowledge on his lips" (Proverbs 14:7).* Do not hang out with them and allow them to pour their filthy, godless conversations into your spirit.

Learn the power of peaceful words. *"Through patience a ruler can be persuaded, and a gentle tongue can break a bone" (Proverbs 25:15).*

Recognize your tongue is a weapon. Your tongue is a weapon you can use to overcome the enemy instead of being defeated by him: *"And they overcame him (Satan) by the blood of the Lamb and by the word of their testimony..." (Revelation 12:11, KJV).*

Avoid these communication errors which the Bible warns against.

-Murmuring and complaining: Complaining is actually a form of rebellion against God. When the nation of Israel complained against Moses and Aaron, God said they were actually complaining against Him. When you complain, you are rebelling against the way He is doing things and the circumstances He is allowing in your life.   Rebellion is compared to the sin of witchcraft in the Bible (1 Samuel 15:23).   As He did with Israel, God will execute judgment against those who murmur and complain (June 15-16).

-Profanity: Profanity is language or behavior that shows disrespect for God, Jesus, or the Holy Spirit including misuse of their names. It is vulgar and irreverent language or behavior, including jokes or innuendos that mock that which is holy.

-Covetous words*: "Keep your lives free from the love of money and be content with what you have..." (Hebrews 13:5).* See also "covetousness" in this database.

-Idol words: *"But I say unto you, that every idle word that men shall speak, they shall give account thereof in the day of judgment" (Matthew 12:36, KJV).*

-Foolish words: *"The discerning heart seeks knowledge, but the mouth of a fool feeds on folly" (Proverbs 15:14).*

-Unprofitable words: *"Keep reminding them of these things. Warn them before God against quarreling about words; it is of no value, and only ruins those who listen" (2 Timothy 2:14)*

-Fables and commandments of men: *"Not giving heed to Jewish fables, and commandments of men, that turn from the truth" (Titus 1:14, KJV).*

-Evil about things you do not know: *"But these, like natural brute beasts made to be caught and destroyed, speak evil of the things they do not understand, and will utterly perish in their own corruption" (2 Peter 2:12, NKJV).*

-Flattering words: *"You know we never used flattery, nor did we put on a mask to cover up greed--God is our witness. We were not looking for praise from men, not from you or anyone else" (1 Thessalonians 2:5-6).*

-Vain words: *"They speak vanity every one with his neighbor" (Psalms 12:2, KJV).*

-Proud words*: "...with their mouth they speak proudly" (Psalms 17:10, KJV).* See also "Pride" in this database.

-Enticing words: *"And this I say, lest any man should beguile you with enticing words"* (Colossians 2:4, KJV).   Enticing words are words that sound wise and plausible, but are not.

-Boastful words: *"How long shall they utter and speak hard things? And all the workers of iniquity boast themselves"* (Psalms 94:4, KJV).

-Words that misuse God's name: *"You shall not misuse the name of the Lord your God, for the Lord will not hold anyone guiltless who misuses his name."* (Exodus 20:7).

-Cursing and bitter words: *"Whose mouth is full of cursing and bitterness"* (Romans 3:14, KJV).

-Lies: *"Let the lying lips be put to silence, which speak grievous things proudly and contemptuously against the righteous"* (Psalms 31:18, KJV).

-Malicious words against others: *"So if I come, I will call attention to what he is doing, gossiping maliciously about us"* (3 John 10).

-Backbiting words: *"...and has no slander on his tongue, who does his neighbor no wrong and casts no slur on his fellowman"* (Psalms 15:3).

-Words of discord: *"...one who sows discord among brethren"* (Proverbs 6:19, NKJV).

-Contentious words: *"A fool's lips enter into contention, and his mouth calls for blows"* (Proverbs 18:6, NKJV).

-Words of strife: *"You shall hide them in the secret place of Your presence from the plots of man; You shall keep them secretly in a pavilion from the strife of tongues"* (Psalms 31:20, NKJV).

-Devouring and deceitful words: *"You love every harmful word, O you deceitful tongue!"* (Psalms 52:4).

-Froward and perverse words: *"Put away perversity from your mouth; keep corrupt talk far from your lips"* (Proverbs 4:24).

-Mischievous words: *"They also that seek after my life lay snares for me: and they that seek my hurt speak mischievous things and imagine deceits all the day long"* (Psalms 38:12, KJV).

-Tale-bearing words: *"A talebearer reveals secrets, but he who is of a faithful spirit conceals a matter"* (Proverbs 11:13, NKJV).

WHAT GOD'S WORD SAYS ABOUT COMMUNICATION:

You shall not misuse the name of the Lord your God, for the Lord will not hold anyone guiltless who misuses his name. (Exodus 20:7, NIV)

You have tested my heart; You have visited me in the night; You have tried me and have found nothing; I have purposed that my mouth shall not transgress. (Psalms 17:3, NKJV)

Let the words of my mouth, and the meditation of my heart, be acceptable in thy sight, O Lord, my strength, and my redeemer. (Psalms 19:14, KJV)

Keep your tongue from evil and your lips from speaking lies. (Psalms 34:13)

I said, I will take heed to my ways, that I sin not with my tongue: I will keep my mouth with a bridle, while the wicked is before me. (Psalms 39:1, KJV)

"Whoever offers praise glorifies Me; And to him who orders his conduct aright I will show the salvation of God." (Psalms 50:23, NKJV)

Create in me a clean heart, O God; and renew a right spirit within me. (Psalm 51:10, KJV)

You love every harmful word, Oh you deceitful tongue! (Psalm 52:4)

Praise the Lord, you his angels, you mighty ones who do his bidding, who obey his word. (Psalm 103:20)

Set a guard over my mouth, O Lord; keep watch over the door of my lips. (Psalm 141:3)

Put away perversity from your mouth; keep corrupt talk far from your lips. (Proverbs 4:24)
Hear; For I will speak of excellent things; and the opening of my lips shall be right things.

For my mouth shall speak truth; and wickedness is an abomination to my lips. All the words of my mouth are in righteousness; there is nothing froward or perverse in them. (Proverbs 8:6-8, KJV)

The mouth of the righteous is a fountain of life, but overwhelms the mouth of the wicked. (Proverbs 10:11)

When words are many, sin is not absent, but he who holds his tongue is wise. (Proverbs 10:19)

The lips of the righteous nourish many, but fools die for lack of judgment. (Proverbs 10:21)

The words of the wicked lie in wait for blood, but the speech of the upright rescues them. (Proverbs 12:6)

From the fruit of his lips a man is filled with good things as surely as the work of his hands rewards him. (Proverbs 12:14)

Reckless words pierce like a sword, but the tongue of the wise brings healing. (Proverbs 12:18)

The tongue of the wise commends knowledge, but the mouth of the fool gushes folly. (Proverbs 15:2)

A man finds joy in giving an apt reply--and how good is a timely word! (Proverbs 15:23)

The heart of the righteous weighs its answers, but the mouth of the wicked gushes evil. (Proverbs 15:28)

Pleasant words are a honeycomb, sweet to the soul and healing to the bones. (Proverbs 16:24)

Starting a quarrel is like breaching a dam; so drop the matter before a dispute breaks out. (Proverbs 17:14)

A man of knowledge uses words with restraint, and a man of understanding is even-tempered. Even a fool is thought wise if he keeps silent, and discerning if he holds his tongue. (Proverbs 17:27-28)

A fool's mouth is his destruction, and his lips are the snare of his soul. (Proverbs 18:7)

He who answers before listening--that is his folly and his shame. (Proverbs 18:13)

From the fruit of his mouth a man's stomach is filled; with the harvest from his lips he is satisfied. The tongue has the power of life and death. (Proverbs 18:20-21)

He who guards his mouth and his tongue keeps himself from calamity. (Proverbs 21:23)

A word aptly spoken is like apples of gold in settings of silver. (Proverbs 25:11)

Through patience a ruler can be persuaded, and a gentle tongue can break a bone. (Proverbs 25:15)

A fool gives full vent to his anger, but a wise man keeps himself under control. (Proverbs 29:11)

Do you see a man who speaks in haste? There is more hope for a fool than for him. (Proverbs 29:20)

Do not be quick with your mouth, do not be hasty in your heart to utter anything before God. God is in heaven and you are on earth, so let your words be few. (Ecclesiastes 5:2)

Do not let your mouth lead you into sin... (Ecclesiastes 5:6)

The words of the wise are as goads, and as nails fastened by the masters of assemblies, which are given from one shepherd. (Ecclesiastes 12:11, KJV)

Do not pay attention to every word people say. (Ecclesiastes 7:21)

The quiet words of the wise are more to be heeded than the shouts of a ruler of fools. (Ecclesiastes 9:17)

So, shall My word be that goes forth from My mouth; It shall not return to Me void, But it shall accomplish what I please, And it shall prosper in the thing for which I sent it. (Isaiah 55:11, NKJV)

Simply let your 'Yes' be 'Yes,' and your 'No,' 'No'; anything beyond this comes from the evil one. (Matthew 5:37)

Men will have to give account on the day of judgment for every careless word they have spoken. For by your words you will be acquitted, and by your words you will be condemned. (Matthew 12:36-37)

As for you, you were dead in your transgressions and sins, in which you used to live when you followed the ways of this world and of the ruler of the kingdom of the air, the spirit who is now at work in those who are disobedient. All of us also lived among them at one time, gratifying the cravings of our sinful nature and following its desires and thoughts. Like the rest, we were by nature objects of wrath. But because of his great love for us, God, who is rich in mercy, made us alive with Christ even when we were dead in transgressions--it is by grace you have been saved. And God raised us up with Christ and seated us with him in the heavenly realms in Christ Jesus, (Ephesians 2:1-6)

You were taught, with regard to your former way of life, to put off your old self, which is being corrupted by its deceitful desires; to be made new in the attitude of your minds; and to put on the new self, created to be like God in true righteousness and holiness. Therefore, each of you must put off falsehood and speak truthfully to his neighbor, for we are all members of one body. (Ephesians 4:22-25)

Let no corrupt communication proceed out of your mouth, but that which is good to the use of edifying, that it may minister grace unto the hearers. (Ephesians 4:29, KJV)

Let all...evil speaking be put away from you... (Ephesians 4:31, KJV)

But now also put off...filthy communication out of your mouth. (Colossians 3:8, NKJV)

Don't let anyone look down on you because you are young, but set an example for the believers in speech, in life, in love, in faith and in purity. (1 Timothy 4:12)

That the communication of thy faith may become effectual by the acknowledging of every good thing which is in you in Christ Jesus. (Philemon 6, KJV)

My dear brothers, take note of this: Everyone should be quick to listen, slow to speak and slow to become angry, for man's anger does not bring about the righteous life that God desires. Therefore, get rid of all moral filth and the evil that is so prevalent and humbly accept the word planted in you, which can save you. (James 1:19-21)

Likewise, the tongue is a small part of the body, but it makes great boasts. Consider what a great forest is set on fire by a small spark. The tongue also is a fire, a world of evil among the parts of the body. It corrupts the whole person, sets the whole course of his life on fire, and is itself set on fire by hell. All kinds of animals, birds, reptiles and creatures of the sea are being tamed and have been tamed by man, but no man can tame the tongue. It is a restless evil, full of deadly poison. With the tongue we praise our Lord and Father, and with it we curse men, who have been made in God's likeness. Out of the same mouth come praise and cursing. My brothers, this should not be. Can both fresh water and salt water flow from the same spring? My brothers, can a fig tree bear olive, or a grapevine bear fig? Neither can a salt spring produce fresh water. (James 3:6-12)

...be holy in all manner of conversation; Because it is written, be holy; for I am holy. (1 Peter 1:15-16)

For, whoever would love life and see good days must keep his tongue from evil and his lips from deceitful speech. (1 Peter 3:10)

If anyone speaks, he should do it as one speaking the very words of God. (1 Peter 4:11)

CHAPTER TWELVE

The "it: of Unforgiveness and Reconciliation Issues

DEFINITION: Forgiveness is the act of pardoning someone for an offense. Reconciliation is the ending of conflict between two or more people and the renewing of relationship. Included in the biblical concept of forgiveness is receiving forgiveness from God for sin, extending forgiveness to others, and forgiving ones' self. Forgiveness includes the releasing of grudges and bitterness over past offenses.

FACTS ABOUT FORGIVENESS AND RECONCILIATION:

Forgiveness and reconciliation come through Jesus Christ. *"All this is from God, who reconciled us to himself through Christ and gave us the ministry of reconciliation: that God was reconciling the world to himself in Christ, not counting men's sins against them. And he has committed to us the message of reconciliation. We are therefore Christ's ambassadors, as though God were making his appeal through us. We implore you on Christ's behalf: Be reconciled to God" (2 Corinthians 5:18-20).*

God promises forgiveness for your sin. When you confess your sins to God and repent, you are forgiven because He promises this in His Word (1 John 1:8-9). By repenting and accepting the sacrifice of Jesus Christ for your sin, you are reconciled to God. You may not "feel" forgiven, but the Christian walk is by faith not by feeling. God promised, and He cannot lie (Numbers 23:19). Jesus said*: ..."whoever comes to me I will never drive away" (John 6:37).*

Broken relationships result in additional problems. Bitterness, grudges, resentment, anger, etc., all result from broken relationships. These negative emotions affect you mentally, physically, and spiritually. They are all sinful emotions that must be dealt with in order to receive and extend forgiveness.

The Bible teaches forgiveness. You need forgiveness from God and you are required to forgive others (Matthew 6:14-15). You also need to forgive yourself.

DEALING WITH FORGIVENESS AND RECONCILATION:

Be reconciled to God. A proper vertical relationship with God makes positive horizontal relationships with others possible. Confess your sins and ask God to forgive you. Read Psalm 51. You do not need to repeatedly ask forgiveness for a sin. Once you have confessed and asked forgiveness, God forgives and forgets (Isaiah 43:25). Remain reconciled to God by praying the model prayer, designed to be prayed daily, which includes "forgive our sins as we forgive others" (Matthew 6:12).

Repent of your unforgiveness. Repent of bitterness, anger, resentment, and holding grudges. These are all sin and must be dealt with as such.

Forgive others. You may not feel like it, but by an act of your will you must forgive others.
Follow the directives given in Matthew 18:15-19.   Forgiveness is not:
-Justifying someone else's wrongs which they have done to you.
-Denying you were hurt in the first place.
-Accepting with resignation what was done to you.
-Waiting for time to heal the hurt. (It doesn't).

True forgiveness comes by:

-Recognizing what was done to you was wrong, the result of sinful men in a sinful world. It is
not necessary to go back and relive the event mentally, but neither can you deal with it by
denying it. Acknowledge what happened and how it affected you.

-Confessing the hurt to God and asking Him to heal you of the harmful emotions. You may
never forget the facts of the incident, but what is needed is healing for the negative emotions
relating to it.

-Asking God to help you forgive others, even as Christ forgives you.   Recognize that God
extends forgiveness to you as you forgive others: *"Forgive us our trespasses AS we forgive those
who trespass against us."*

If others offend you again, forgive them again. Peter asked Christ how many times he was
required to forgive someone. Jesus answered: *"I tell you, not seven times, but seventy-seven
times" (Matthew 18:21-22).* He was actually saying that your forgiveness must be unlimited.

Forgive yourself. Distinguish between true remorse and guilt and shame. You are right to feel
remorse, but guilt and shame are not from God. Jesus bore your sins, your guilt, and your shame
on the cross (Hebrews 12:2). You do not have to bear these things (1 John 3:20). If you have
confessed your sin to God and sought forgiveness and reconciliation with others, then you must
also forgive yourself. See yourself as God sees you, a new creature in Christ (2 Corinthians
5:17). Here are some guidelines to help you forgive yourself.

-Acknowledge the sin that is causing your feelings of guilt. Confess your sin to God, and repent.
Ask God to forgive your sin and heal your emotions.

-Recognize when God forgives, He forgets--He casts your sins as far as east from west (Psalm
103:12).

-Claim the promises of 1 John 1:8-9 and Romans 8:1.

-By an act of your own will, release yourself from condemnation. Control future thoughts by
casting down "vain imaginations" of guilt and shame and "forgetting those things behind" (2
Corinthians 10:5 and Philippians 3:3).

WHAT GOD'S WORD SAYS ABOUT FORGIVENESS AND RECONCILIATION:

Blessed is he whose transgressions are forgiven, whose sins are covered. (Psalm 32:1)

Read David's prayer of repentance in Psalm 51.

For You, Lord, are good, and ready to forgive, and abundant in mercy to all those who call upon You. (Psalm 86:5)

He hath not dealt with us after our sins, nor rewarded us after our iniquities. For as the heavens are high above the earth, so great is his lovingkindness toward them that fear him. As far as the east is from the west, so far hath he removed our transgressions from us. (Psalm 103:10-12)

Hatred stirs up strife, but love covers all sins. (Proverbs 10:12)

He who conceals his sins does not prosper, but whoever confesses and renounces them finds mercy. (Proverbs 28:13)

"Come now, let us reason together," says the Lord."Though your sins are like scarlet, they shall be as white as snow; though they are red as crimson, they shall be like wool." (Isaiah 1:18)

Forget the former things; do not dwell on the past. (Isaiah 43:18)

"I, even I, am he who blots out your transgressions, for my own sake, and remembers your sins no more." (Isaiah 43:25)

But he was wounded for our transgressions, he was bruised for our iniquities: the chastisement of our peace was upon him; and with his stripes we are healed. All we like sheep have gone astray; we have turned everyone to his own way; and the Lord hath laid on him the iniquity of us all. (Isaiah 53:5-6)

"Therefore, if you are offering your gift at the altar and there remember that your brother has something against you, leave your gift there in front of the altar. First go and be reconciled to your brother; then come and offer your gift." (Matthew 5:23-24)

Forgive us our debts, as we also have forgiven our debtors. (Matthew 6:12)

For if you forgive men when they sin against you, your heavenly Father will also forgive you. But if you do not forgive men their sins, your Father will not forgive your sins. (Matthew 6:14-15)

If your brother sins against you, go and show him his fault, just between the two of you. If he listens to you, you have won your brother over. But if he will not listen, take one or two others along, so that every matter may be established by the testimony of two or three witnesses. If he refuses to listen to them, tell it to the church; and if he refuses to listen even to the church, treat him as you would a pagan or a tax collector. (Matthew 18:15-17)

Then Peter came to Jesus and asked, "Lord, how many times shall I forgive my brother when he sins against me? Up to seven times?" Jesus answered, "I tell you, not seven times, but seventy-seven times." (Matthew 18:21-22)

The parable about forgiveness in Matthew 18:23-35 illustrates how your forgiveness by God is related to forgiving others.

And when you stand praying, if you hold anything against anyone, forgive him, so that your Father in heaven may forgive you your sins. (Mark 11:25-26)

But I tell you who hear me: Love your enemies, do good to those who hate you, bless those who curse you, pray for those who mistreat you. If someone strikes you on one cheek, turn to him the other also. If someone takes your cloak, do not stop him from taking your tunic. Give to everyone who asks you, and if anyone takes what belongs to you, do not demand it back. Do to others as you would have them do to you. (Luke 6:27-31)

Forgive, and you will be forgiven. (Luke 6:37)

All that the Father gives me will come to me, and whoever comes to me I will never drive away. (John 6:37)

A new commandment I give to you, that you love one another; as I have loved you, that you also love one another. By this all will know that you are My disciples, if you have love for one another. (John 13:34-35)

Repent, then, and turn to God, so that your sins may be wiped out, that times of refreshing may come from the Lord. (Acts 3:19)

Blessed are those whose lawless deeds are forgiven, and whose sins are covered; Blessed is the man to whom the Lord shall not impute sin. (Romans 4:7-8)

Therefore, since we have been justified through faith, we have peace with God through our Lord Jesus Christ, through whom we have gained access by faith into this grace in which we now stand. (Romans 5:1)

There is therefore now no condemnation to those who are in Christ Jesus, who do not walk according to the flesh, but according to the Spirit. (Romans 8:1)

All this is from God, who reconciled us to himself through Christ and gave us the ministry of reconciliation: that God was reconciling the world to himself in Christ, not counting men's sins against them. And he has committed to us the message of reconciliation. We are therefore Christ's ambassadors, as though God were making his appeal through us. We implore you on Christ's behalf: Be reconciled to God. (2 Corinthians 5:18-20)

In him we have redemption through his blood, the forgiveness of sins, in accordance with the riches of God's grace. (Ephesians 1:7)

...by abolishing in his flesh, the law with its commandments and regulations. His purpose was to create in himself one new man out of the two, thus making peace, and in this one body to reconcile both of them to God through the cross, by which he put to death their hostility. He came and preached peace to you who were far away and peace to those who were near. For through him we both have access to the Father by one Spirit. (Ephesians 2:15-18))

Be completely humble and gentle; be patient, bearing with one another in love. Make every effort to keep the unity of the Spirit through the bond of peace. (Ephesians 4:2-3)

Be kind and compassionate to one another, forgiving each other, just as in Christ God forgave you. (Ephesians 4:32)

For he has rescued us from the dominion of darkness and brought us into the kingdom of the Son he loves, in whom we have redemption, the forgiveness of sins. (Colossians 1:13-14)

For God was pleased to have all his fullness dwell in him, and through him to reconcile to himself all things, whether things on earth or things in heaven, by making peace through his blood, shed on the cross. (Colossians 1:19-20)

Therefore, as God's chosen people, holy and dearly loved, clothe yourselves with compassion, kindness, humility, gentleness and patience. Bear with each other and forgive whatever grievances you may have against one another. Forgive as the Lord forgave you. (Colossians 3:13)

See to it that no one misses the grace of God and that no bitter root grows up to cause trouble and defile many (Hebrews 12:15)

And above all things have fervent love for one another, for "love will cover a multitude of sins." (1 Peter 4:8)

If we claim to be without sin, we deceive ourselves and the truth is not in us. If we confess our sins, he is faithful and just and will forgive us our sins and purify us from all unrighteousness. If we claim we have not sinned, we make him out to be a liar and his word has no place in our lives. (1 John 1:8-10)

CONCLUSION

How to Get Rid of "it" though Personal Deliverance

When you understand self-deliverance, you will keep yourself from being bond; you will keep yourself healthy, physically and spiritually and be free from spiritual pollution. Every day, you will enjoy divine health and will not be spending your money on drugs and hospital bills.

Sometimes, there may not be a minister who is anointed and knowledgeable about deliverance to help you. Sometimes, you can be heavily attacked and the next service is about four days away. What do you do? You should never allow evil spirits to reside in your life. If you lack adequate time to do a self-deliverance in the mornings, after your quiet time, then, when you're having your bath, you could do it.

Whatever the causes of our spiritual afflictions, there are several proven steps we may try to help ourselves find freedom and healing. If these steps do not resolve your situation, then perhaps it is time to ask for help:

Step 1 — Conversion

Deliverance from any level of bondage, or harassment (collectively called, "spiritual afflictions") cannot be achieved without personal conversion. Deliverance from milder forms of spiritual affliction may often be achieved by the various acts of personal conversion—Acts of Contrition, Faith, Hope, Charity, and Consecration. "Prayer Acts" and other prayers, with fasting, and various devotions are often effective to drive evil spirits away:

So humble yourselves before God. Resist the Devil, and he will flee from you. Draw close to God, and God will draw close to you. — (James 4:7,8)

The first step, therefore, is make up your mind to live the Christ-life; or if already doing so, to persevere in living the Christ-life. This internal conversion, which is a conscious decision and determination to follow Christ and all of His teachings, precedes all other steps to deliverance. Without conversion to the Faith in Jesus Christ and participation in His family, the Church, deliverance, even if seemingly effective for a while, cannot be successful in the long run. It is the *"Truth"* that makes us free (John 8:31b), not prayers, rituals, counseling, or personal will in themselves. It is the confrontation with Truth that sends the demons running back to hell. This is why the method of Deliverance Counseling we use is called a *"Truth Encounter"*. As demons are confronted with the Truth, and as we are confronted with the Truth, of whom we are in Christ, we gain freedom. The foundation of all truth is Jesus Christ, who is Truth (John 14:6). Without our Lord Jesus Christ, we can never know truth or obtain it.

Some people believe they are unable to make a profession of faith in Jesus Christ. In such cases the person should ask God for help—ask Him for the faith that will save, deliver, and heal.

If we are willing to accept the gift of faith from God, our Lord will give it to us when we ask:

And I tell you, Ask, and it will be given you; seek, and you will find; knock, and it will be opened to you. For every one who asks receives, and he who seeks finds, and to him who knocks it will be opened. What father among you, if his son asks for a fish, will instead of a fish give him a serpent; or if he asks for an egg, will give him a scorpion? If you then, who are evil, know how to give good gifts to your children, how much more will the heavenly Father give the Holy Spirit to those who ask him! — (Luke 11:9-13)

Sincerely ask God for the faith that brings saving faith, the faith of conversion to the One, that is Jesus Christ, whom who declares:

I am the way, and the truth, and the life; no one comes to the Father, but by me (John 14:6) .... Come to me, all who labor and are heavy laden, and I will give you rest (Matthew 11:28) .... I will not reject anyone who comes to me (John 6:37) .... [rather] take my yoke upon you, and learn from me; for I am gentle and lowly in heart, and you will find rest for your souls. For my yoke is easy, and my burden is light (Matt 11:29-30)

Step 2 — Repentance

Essential to growing closer to God in faith, devotion, and love is to repent of those behaviors, desires, beliefs, and ideas that are sinful. The definition of sin is much broader than most people imagine. A definition of sin:

Sin is an offense against reason, truth, and right conscience; it is a failure in genuine love for God and neighbor caused by a perverse attachment to certain goods. Its wounds the nature of man and injures human solidarity. It has been defined as "an utterance, a deed, or a desire contrary to the eternal law."

Sin is an offense against God: *"Against you, you alone, have I sinned, and done that which is evil in your sight"* (Ps 51:4). Sin sets itself against God's love for us and turns our hearts away from it. Like the first sin (of Adam and Eve), it is disobedience, a revolt against God through the will to become "like gods" (Gen 3:5), knowing and determining good and evil. Sin is thus "love of oneself even to contempt of God." In this proud self-exaltation, sin is diametrically opposed to the obedience of Jesus, which achieves our salvation (cf. Phil 2:6-9).

We must repent of our sin, but repentance involves more than merely "turning away" from sin. Repentance must also renounce all that opposes God and all that He finds sinful. This includes renouncing Satan and his ways, renouncing personal sins, and renouncing all that leads us to sin. Some of the common sins and situations that interfere with deliverance include: involvement in non-Christian activities like the occult; persistent situational sins such as living together without marriage or remarriage without annulment of previous marriages; maintaining improper or problematic friendships; illegal activities of any sort; and sins that have become habitual such as pornography, masturbation, fornication, gossip, lying, stealing, etc.

The three greatest stumbling blocks to deliverance is Pride, Rebellion, and Unforgiveness and all the things that go along with those three sins. Repentance of Pride, Rebellion, and Unforgiveness is required to even hope for deliverance. Repentance also includes the firm amendment to avoid sin, and the near occasion of sin, in the future. Repentance requires a *complete* turnaround of our lives, a becoming a *"new man"*, so that...

...you should put away the old self of your former way of life, corrupted through deceitful desires, and be renewed in the spirit of your minds, and put on the new self, created in God's way in righteousness and holiness of truth. Therefore, putting away falsehood, speak the truth, each one to his neighbor, for we are members one of another...(thus) do not leave room for the devil (Eph 4:22-25,26b)

Step 3 — Confession

With faith and contrition of heart, repentance of mind, firm purpose to avoid sin and that which leads us to sin, we must now confess our sins before our God who is a God of forgiveness and mercy. This is a critical step that we will discuss at length.

The manner of our confession differs, but within our respective traditions, confession is required:

If we confess our sins, he is faithful and just, and will forgive our sins and cleanse us from all unrighteousness. (1 John 1:9)

... if you confess with your mouth that Jesus is Lord and believe in your heart that God raised him from the dead, you will be saved. For one believes with the heart and so is justified, and one confesses with the mouth and so is saved. (Romans 10:9-10)

 "Confess your sins to each other and pray for each other so that you may be healed. The earnest prayer of a righteous person has great power and wonderful results" (James 5:16).

This confidant maybe one's pastor or another minister, or a trusted friend. We must be careful when choosing an "accountability partner." Since we will be revealing very private and sensitive information about ourselves, it is critically important to trust whoever we choose as a confidant to be discreet and to keep absolutely confidential the information we tell them.

There is wisdom in presenting oneself to an "accountability partner." Personal accountability is upheld when we confess to another person whom may hold us accountable for our actions. Confessing our sins to one another is a powerful way to break the bonds of sin in our lives. It is much harder to confess our sins to one another than to simply say, *"Lord, forgive me"*. While God is forgiving, of course, it is the demands of personal accountability before another human being that brings our confession into grounded reality that strengthens our commitment to turn away from sin in the future.

Religious ministers, psychologists, counselors, and others including the Deliverance Counselors of agency, are also bound either by law, ethical codes, or contract with the client (or bound by any combination thereof) to keep private and confidential all that is revealed to them. In addition, those in the ministerial and helping professions are usually trained in the ethics, legalities, and culture of maintaining confidentiality. They are use to keeping private the personal information of their patients and clients. Friends, on the other hand, may not have such training and may not be use to the culture of confidentiality. Thus, if one's confidant is not a pastor, or at least a minister, psychologist, or counselor bound by law and/or ethical codes, take care to ensure the chosen confidant understands thoroughly that he must keep private all that he hears and may not discuss it with anyone, not even with his spouse.

There is a great psychological comfort in hearing the words, "I forgive you" or the equivalent, "I absolve you of your sins." Our Father in heaven understands this psychological need. Thus, in His great love for us, He provided a way for us to hear those words in His name. It is God who ultimately forgives sins, but God, according to His sovereign authority chose to delegate this authority to His validly ordained priests. This power was given to the Apostles in John 20:22-23 and was passed on from them to those whom they appointed.

Our Father in heaven also knows and understands our need to be a family and for the family to come to our aid when we are hurting, to offer forgiveness when we fall, and to provide healing and strength to help us grow in faith. God forgives you when you appeal to Him with your heart-felt and sincere repentance and confession. Follow the tradition of your denomination and always offer a prayer for forgiveness as soon as possible after sinning. Then, in obedience to the Bible, seek accountability by confession to a confidant to complete your healing.

Step 4 — Removing the Greatest Stumbling blocks: Pride, Rebellion, and Forgiveness

We have already mentioned that the three biggest stumbling blocks to deliverance is usually Pride, Rebellion, and Unforgiveness. These three sins distance us from God. To draw closer to God we need to give up our pride, obey our Lord's teachings, and forgive those who hurt us.

In Deliverance Counseling we help our clients through exercises to locate pockets of pride and rebellion and to rid themselves of these sins with the help of God through prayer. Forgiveness, however, tends to be the most difficult, partly because of pride or even rebellion perhaps, but mostly because of deeply emotional issues surrounding the circumstances of the hurts someone has given us. Whatever the causes of our unforgiveness, deliverance is not possible until we can come to forgive, thus we shall discuss this topic at some length too.

The following guide is rather long, but this step is one of the most important. One simple MUST deals with Pride, Rebellion, and Unforgiveness if deliverance and healing is to be permanently possible.

Pride: Pride is the essential sin that leads to most other sins. It is the sin of Lucifer that led him to rebel against God resulting in his expulsion from heaven and becoming Satan.

Pride is a killer. Pride says, "I can do it! I can get myself out of this mess without God and without anyone else's helped." No, we can't! We absolutely need God, and we desperately need each other.

Pride also says "I know the best and most efficient way and how dare others get in the way of that" or "How dare things not go my way" or "How dare some person or something get in the way of what I want to do." Impatience is a factor of pride. Other ways impatience reveals our pride is getting impatient when we cannot find our car keys, or when we are late to a meeting, or if someone is driving too slowly for us on the hi-way, or when the computer acts up and interrupts our train of thought.

Impatience is the sister to Pride because it is caused essentially by our desire to have things our own way, in our own time, and according to our own preferences.

Pride is also the engine behind egotism (thinking more of oneself than one ought) and behind false humility (putting oneself down to be less than what one actually is). Pride is the force behind resistance to lawful and appropriate authority — whether that authority is a parent, teacher, police officer, government, employer, or the Church.

Pride is the basis of thinking of oneself as better than others, being pompous, and having contempt toward one's neighbors, employers, other family members, or the Church and her ministers.

Pride can also rear its ugly head in more subtle ways such as reluctance to apologize when we need to apologize, demanding our rights merely because it is our right, being inappropriately unkind or rude, jealousy, being quick-tempered, moodiness, brooding over wrongs done by others to oneself, depression and despair, or demanding that we are right about something, when indeed we are right about the issue, even though the issue is unimportant or can be handled differently (this is a major phenomenon in marriages, families, and friendships — the phrase "We need to choose our battles" is an important remedy for this).

Other ways that Pride expresses itself include: by taking personal credit for gifts or possessions and thus refusing to acknowledge that we have what we have by God's Providence; glorying in our achievements as if they were not primary a result of God's grace and divine goodness; by minimizing one's defeats; by claiming qualities that are not actually possessed; magnifying the faults and defects of others or dwelling upon the defects and faults of others.

James 4:6-10 and 1 Peter 5:1-10 reveals that spiritual conflict follows pride.

Examine yourself for these and any other attributes of pride and then pray:

Dear Heavenly Father. You have said that pride goes before destruction and an arrogant spirit before stumbling (Prov. 16:18). I confess that I have not denied myself, picked up my cross daily, and followed You (Matt. 16:24). In so doing I have given ground to the enemy in my life. I have believed that I could be successful and live victoriously by my own strength and resources. I now confess that I have sinned against You by placing my will before You and by centering my life around self instead of You.

I now renounce the self-life and by so doing cancel all the ground that has been gained in my life by the enemies of the Lord Jesus Christ. I pray that You will guide me so that I will do nothing from selfishness or empty conceit, but with humility of mind that I will regard others as more important than myself (Phil. 2:3). Enable me through love to serve others and in honor prefer others (Rom. 12:10). Amen.

Rebellion: We often place our confidence in the flesh not only with the "I can do it myself" attitude but each time we assert our own opinions above the teachings of Christ. It is a pride and a rebellion to say, "I want to do it my way" or "I want to think the way I want" without regard to the ways God teaches us to go and to believe. This is an arrogance that not only can get us into major trouble but also forms a major vulnerability for demons to come into our life.

Rebelling against God and His authority gives Satan an opportunity to attack. As our commanding general, the Lord Jesus Christ says, *"Get into ranks and follow Me. I will not lead you into temptation, but I will deliver you from evil."*

The Bible teaches us that it is the will of God for us to be obedient to parents, to civil government, to the Church, and to the pastors who are over us. We have two biblical responsibilities in regard to these authority figures: 1) Pray for them; and 2) submit to them. The only time God permits us to disobey those in authority over us is when they require of us an act or acquiescence in ways that are contrary to Church Law, Natural Law, or Divine Law.

Being under authority is an act of faith; we are trusting God to work through His established lines of authority. The authority that God has ordained does not mean, however, that we are to submit to abuse from those authorities. In those cases where someone in authority over us is abusing us in any way, then we need to act in appropriate ways according to the situation — such as appeal to the state for protection and relief for civil or criminal issues; or appeal to Church authorities on some issue involving religion or our parish; or make appropriate decisions such as terminating an abusive relationship, etc. Whoever the authority, who is abusing, we need to pray for the offender and to forgive him; but we are not required to be a doormat or target of their abuse.

Some of the lines of authority mentioned in the Bible include:

- Church leaders (Hebrews 13:17; Matthew 18:15-18)
- Parents (Ephesians 6: 1-3; Exodus 20:12)
- Husbands (1 Peter 3:1-3; Ephesians 5:23-24)
- Employers (1 Peter 2:18-21)
- Civil Government (Romans 13:1-5; 1 Timothy 2:1-3; 1 Peter 2:13-16)

Examine yourself for any areas of rebellion (deliberate driving faster than the speed limit is rebellion, too, you know!) and then pray:

Dear Heavenly Father. You have said that rebellion is as the sin of witchcraft and insubordination is as iniquity and idolatry (1 Sam. 15.23). I know that in action and attitude I have sinned against You with a rebellious heart. I ask Your forgiveness for my rebellion and pray that by the shed blood of the Lord Jesus Christ, strengthened by intercession of the that all ground gained by evil spirits because of my rebelliousness be canceled and taken back. I pray that You will shed light on all my ways that I may know the full extent of my rebelliousness, and I now choose to adopt a submissive spirit and a servant's heart. Amen.

Unforgiveness: Jesus Himself discusses the seriousness of failing to forgive. He tells us that failure to forgive those who hurt us will result in our not being forgiven ourselves by God. *"Forgive us our trespasses (sins) as we forgive those who trespass (sin) against us"*. The *Our Father*, the Lord's Prayer, which most all of us know and pray, Jesus teaches us that God will be as forgiving to us as we are to others.

Indeed, how can we expect God to forgive us when we do not forgive our brothers? Consider the follow teachings from Holy Scripture:

If you forgive those who sin against you, your heavenly Father will forgive you. But if you refuse to forgive others, your Father will not forgive your sins (Matthew 6:14,15).

But when you are praying, first forgive anyone you are holding a grudge against, so that your Father in heaven will forgive your sins, too (Mark 11:25).

If you forgive others, you will be forgiven. (Luke 6:37b)

Forgiveness is not about emotions and feelings. You can still be hurting, angry and upset and still decide to forgive. Forgiveness involves a mental decision, a decision of will, an act of your free will, even though you may not "Feel it".

The true nature of forgiveness:

1. **Forgiveness is not forgetting:** People who try to forget find that cannot. It is an unfortunate quirk of the English language with the phrase, "Forgive and forget". In actuality this phrase does not mean to "forget" in the sense of not remembering what happened; of course, we will remember. God says He will "remember our sins no more" (Heb. 10: 17), but God, being omniscient, obviously cannot literally forget. "Remember no more" means that God will never use the past against us (Ps. 103:12).

   To forget is really "to let go". We need to *"let go and let God"*. We let go of the past, but more importantly we let go of the hurt. As long as we do not forgive, as long as we do not let go, we allow the offender of our wounds continue to hurt us.

2. **Forgiveness is a choice not a feeling:** Since God requires us to forgive, <u>it is something we can do</u>. God will NEVER ask us to do something that is impossible for us to do; that would be cruel and God is a loving God.

   Forgiveness, however, is difficult for us because it pulls against our feelings and emotional hurts. Forgiveness is not about forgetting our feelings or our emotional hurts. We often will not "feel" like forgiving, but we must forgive anyway. As the Lord Prayer teaches us, God forgives us "as we forgive others". But how can God require this of us when we have been hurt so badly?

   God does not expect your feelings and emotional hurts to be healed overnight. He knows and understands our feelings and our hurts. He is a compassionate God and will help us to heal over time, as we are able. What God expects of us is not an immediate emotional healing, but a decision of will to forgive, a decision of will to trust Him to take care of the offender and to heal us, a decision of will to ask God for, and to commit to, being healed of our wounds.

3. **Forgiveness is not letting the person off the hook:** Forgiving is about you letting go, but it is not letting the offender off the hook. He will still pay for what he did, either before the Law or before God or both.

   Forgiving is surely difficult for us because it pulls against our concept of justice. We want revenge for offenses suffered. But we are told never to take our own revenge (Rom. 12:9). Revenge does more damage to us than it punishes the offender. God's justice will prevail, no one can escape it. Never fear, those who hurt us will be held accountable, but we must let God deal with it. In order for God to deal with it, we need to let Him deal with it by letting go.

   "Why should I let them off the hook?" But doing that is precisely the problem — we are still hooked to them, still bound by our past when we do not forgive.

   To forgive does not mean letting the person off the hook; it means letting yourself off the hook.

4. **But you don't understand how much this person hurt me:** The problem is that when we do not forgive we, in essence, allow the person to still hurt us! The question is, "How do we stop the pain?" The answer is **to forgive!**

   It is important to understand that we do not forgive someone for their sake; we do it for our sake so we can be free. Our need to forgive is not an issue between the offender and us; it is between us and God.

5. **Forgiveness is agreeing to live with the consequences of another's sin:** Forgiveness is costly. We pay the price of the evil we forgive. We are going to live with those consequences whether we want to or not; our only choice is whether or not we will do so in the slavery of bitterness and unforgiveness or with the freedom of forgiveness.

   Jesus took the consequences of our sin upon Himself. All true forgiveness is substitution because no one really forgives without bearing the consequences of the other person's sin. God the Father *"made Him who knew no sin to be sin on our behalf, that we might become the righteousness of God in Him"* (2 Cor. 5:2 1).

   Where is the justice? We might ask. It is the Cross that makes forgiveness legally and morally right: *"For the death that He died, He died to sin, once for all"* (Rom. 6: 10). This doesn't mean that we tolerate sin. We must always stand against sin, but we must give the offender to God and get on with our life.

6. **How do we forgive from our heart?** First, we acknowledge the hurt and the hate. If our forgiveness does not visit the emotional core of our life, it will be incomplete. Many feel the pain of interpersonal offenses, but they will not

acknowledge it. Let God bring the pain to the surface so He can deal with it. This is where the healing takes place.

Do not wait to forgive until we feel like forgiving; we will never get there. Feelings take time to heal mostly <u>after</u> the choice to forgive is made and Satan has lost his place (Eph. 4:26, 27). Freedom is what will be gained, not a feeling.

7. **Summary of Points on Forgiveness:**
    - Forgiveness is necessary to have fellowship with God.
    - It is not forgetting.
    - It is a choice.
    - Letting the offender off <u>our</u> hook is what frees us.
    - The offender is not off God's hook.
    - God says, "Revenge is mine."
    - You must acknowledge the hurt and the hate.
    - Forgiveness means we are agreeing to live with the consequences of another's sin — which we have to do anyway.
    - The justice is in the cross.
    - Choice is between the slavery of bitterness or the freedom of forgiveness.
    - Forgiveness means not using the past against the offender.
    - Forgiveness <u>does not</u> mean tolerating the sin or abuse.
    - Why forgive? To stop the pain! As we live in unforgiveness the offender still hurts us!
    - The issue of forgiveness is between you and God only.
    - The act of forgiveness is for your sake, and for your freedom.

Think about the people in your life for whom you need to forgive, people to whom you hold bitterness, people who have hurt you or disappointed you in anyway, or for whom you hold any kind of grudge. Be sure to ALWAYS include your parents, siblings, spouse, and YOURSELF. There is always something to forgive in our families and in ourselves.

Record all the names you can think of on a sheet of paper and a brief note as to why you need to forgive them. If you do not remember names, list them by what you do remember, such as "the guy in sixth grade with the red hat". If you cannot remember why you need to forgive someone on your list that is okay; forgive them for whatever it was — God knows.

After preparing this list ask God to bring to your mind anyone you have forgotten. It is not unusual to forget, or to push aside from our conscious mind, incidents and even the names of people whom have hurt us. These hidden hurts and wounds need to be healed as well. Thus, ask God to bring to your mind any person you have forgotten for whom you need to forgive, for whom you hold a grudge against, for which you are bitter, for those who have hurt you, with the following prayer:

Father in heaven, please bring to my mind the names of any people for whom I have held bitterness towards, grudges against, or have not forgiven for the hurts they have caused me. Help me to remember all these hurts so that they may be offered to You, O Lord, and healed from my soul so that I may live the truly victorious Christ-life. Amen.

Add to your list the names of anyone God may bring to your mind.

Now it is time to pray...

The following prayer needs to be said for each person on the list for which you need to forgive. Do not go to the next person on the list until you are sure you have dealt with all the remembered pain.

As you pray, God may bring to your mind various offending people and experiences that has been totally forgotten. Allow God to do this even if it is painful. Remember this process of forgiveness is for your sake because God wants you to be free.

Remember also that by forgiving the offender we are not rationalizing or trying to explain the offender's behavior. Forgiveness deals with the victim's pain, your pain, not another's excuses. Positive feelings will follow in time; freeing you from the past is the critical issue now.

If you are willing to forgive for your sake, so that you can walk away from this webpage free in Christ, free from the past and from person who hurt you, pray the introductory prayer below and then pray the "Prayer to Forgive" for each person on your list:

Heavenly Father, I now ask for your help in forgiving all those people on my list. Although I am still hurt and angry with them, I know that they are your children and that you love them more than I can possibly know. For this reason, my God, I ask you to help me forgive them. I lay down all bitterness, resentment and hatred for this person and I freely choose to forgive them. Teach me to be more merciful, my God, and help me be always willing, just as you are always willing, to forgive those who sin against me. Amen."

Prayer to Forgive

Lord, I forgive ________________________________ for (specifically identify all offenses and painful memories).

May God heal you and bless you!

Step 5 — Know Who You Are in Christ!

In order to gain freedom, it is important to know who you are in Christ. Thus, you need to evaluate the concept you have of yourself, to acknowledge the truth about God and about yourself; about your relationship and ideas about God and about the manner of our lives.

We often deceive ourselves about our position in Christ and our relationship with Him. For example, we may say to ourselves: "This isn't going to work" or "I wish I could believe this but I can't" or perhaps even more direct deceptions or denials concerning the promises of God for His children. Areas of deception that we may have include:

1. **Self-Deception** (telling ourselves things that are not true)

- o Listening to God's words but thinking we do not have to do it (Ja 1:22; 4:17)
- o Thinking we have no sin or do not sin (1 Jn 1:8)
- o Thinking that we are something when we are not (Gal 6:3)
- o Believing that we will not reap what we sow (Gal 6:7)
- o Thinking we are wise and sophisticated in the 21st century (1 Cor 3:18, 19)
- o Believing that the unrighteous will reach heaven (1 Cor 6:9)
- o Thinking we can associate with bad company and not be corrupted (1 Cor 15:33)

2. **Self-Defense** (defending ourselves instead of trusting Christ)
   - o Denial (conscious or subconscious)
   - o Fantasy (escape from the real world)
   - o Emotional insulation (withdraw to avoid rejection)
   - o Regression (reverting back to a less threatening time in the past)
   - o Displacement (taking out frustrations on others)
   - o Projection (blaming others or accusing others of things we ourselves have done)
   - o Rationalization (defending self though verbal excursion)

To counter these and other deceptions we tell ourselves we need to exercise faith. Faith is the response to Truth and believing the truth is a CHOICE (not a feeling). If we say, "I want to believe God, but I just can't," then we are deceiving ourselves. Of course, we can believe God. We know that God does not lie. Faith is something we DECIDE to do; it is not something we FEEL like doing. Believing the truth does not make it true; rather it is TRUE, therefore we believe it.

Examine yourself and how you may deceive yourself with "self-deceptions" and "Self-Defense" mechanisms. The pray the following prayer: ...

Prayer to Know the Truth:

Dear Heavenly Father. I know that You desire truth in the inner self and that facing this truth is the way of liberation (John 8:32). I acknowledge that I have been deceived by the father of lies (John 8:44) and that I have deceived myself (1 John 1:8). I pray in the name of the Lord Jesus Christ, and since by faith I have received You into my life and am now seated with Christ in the heavenliest (Eph 2:6), I ask you Father to command all deceiving spirits to depart from me. I now ask You to *"search me, O God, and know my heart: try me and know my anxious thoughts; and see if there be any hurtful way in me, and lead me in the everlasting way"* (Ps. 139:23, 24) In the name of Christ Jesus I pray. Amen.

Knowing the truth about oneself, overcoming self-deceptions and the mechanism of self-defense that hide who we really are, includes understanding our faith in Christ. It is by Christ that our lives have meaning and substance.

The following prayer is the substance of that faith:

Affirmations

I believe that I am a child of God (1 Jn. 3:1-3) and that I am seated with Christ in the heavenlies (Eph. 2:6). I believe that I was saved by the grace of God through faith that is a gift and not the result of my own efforts or merits (Eph 2:8).

I choose to be strong in the Lord and in the strength of His might (Eph 6:10). I put no confidence in the flesh (Phil 3:3) for the weapons of warfare are not of the flesh (2 Cor. 10:4). I put on the whole armor of God (Eph. 6:10-20), and I resolve to stand firm in my faith and to resist the evil one.

I believe that Jesus Christ has all authority in heaven and on earth (Matt 28:18) and that He is the head over all rule and authority (Col 2:10). I believe that Satan and his demons and wicked spirits are subject to the Lord Jesus Christ and therefore to me in Christ since I am a member of Christ's body (Eph 1:19-23).

I believe that apart from Christ I can do nothing (John 15:5) so I declare my dependence upon Him.

I choose to abide in Christ in order to bear much fruit and to glorify the Lord (Jn 15:8) and to accomplish the work of sanctification that Christ began in me through the Cross (James 2).

I believe that since I am a member go God's royal family I have the authority, in the name of Christ Jesus, to ask the Father to command the devil to leave my presence, as I obey the command to resist the devil (James 4:7).

I reject any counterfeit gifts or works of Satan and his minions in my life.

I believe that the truth will set me free (John 8:32) and that walking in the light is the only path of fellowship and freedom (1 John 1:7). Therefore, as a royal member of God's household, I stand against Satan's deceptions by affirming all the doctrines of the Faith and by taking every thought captive in obedience to Christ (2 Cor 10:5).

I declare that the Bible and the Church are the only authoritative standards for me (2 Tim 3:15, 16).

I choose to speak the truth in love (Eph 4:15).

I choose to present my body as an instrument of righteousness, a living and holy sacrifice, and thus I renew my mind daily by the living Word of God in order that I may prove that the will of God is good, acceptable, and perfect (Rom 6:13; 12:1, 2).

I ask my heavenly Father to fill me with His Holy Spirit (Eph 5:18), to lead me into all truth (John 16:13), and to empower my life that I may live above sin and not carry out the desires of the flesh (Gal 5:16). I crucify the flesh (Gal 5:24) and choose to walk by the Spirit.

In making all these affirmations, I renounce all selfish goals and choose the ultimate goal of love (1 Tim 1:5). I choose to obey the greatest commandment to love the Lord my God will all my heart, soul, and mind, and to love my neighbor as myself (Matt 22:37-39). Amen.

Step 6 — Worship, Pray, and Fast

Worship as a Church Family: One of Satan's favorite lies, apart from having us believe that he does not exist, or that he does exist and is more powerful than he truly is, is that since God is everywhere and we can worship Him anywhere and do not need the "community of believers ", the Church family.

Although it is true that God is everywhere and worshiping Him anywhere is wholesome and good, it is false to believe that the Church is unnecessary. Since the earliest days of Christianity, communities of believers gathered together on the *Lord's Day* (Sunday).

Scripture is very clear on the subject of Church attendance and on how our submission to its authority is not only good but required. The Church, its leaders and members, are the Mystical Body of Christ here on Earth. To disobey the teachings of the Church as it relates to faith and morals is to disobey the teachings of Christ. To not attend church is also disobedience to Christ.

Paul admonishes those who do not come to Church in Hebrews 10:19-25:

Therefore, brothers, since through the blood of Jesus we have confidence of entrance into the sanctuary by the new and living way he opened for us through the veil, that is, his flesh, and since we have "a great priest over the house of God," let us approach with a sincere heart and in absolute trust, with our hearts sprinkled clean from an evil conscience and our bodies washed in pure water. Let us hold unwaveringly to our confession that gives us hope, for he who made the promise is trustworthy. We must consider how to rouse one another to love and good works. We should not stay away from our assembly, as is the custom of some, but encourage one another, and this all the more as you see the day drawing near.

Hebrews 13:17

Obey your leaders and submit to them; for they are keeping watch over your souls, as men who will have to give account. Let them do this joyfully, and not sadly, for that would be of no advantage to you.

Worship and prayer together as a family, prayer meetings, adoration, and other corporate settings, and in the privacy of the family at home is critical in developing spiritual health for the family and each family member. Such family devotion forms the foundation for all that each family does away from home in the world of school, work, and society.

Prayer is so important both in the family context and individually. It is important not just because prayer is something a Christian ought to do, but because prayer is communication.

The more we depend on God, the closer He is to us and we are to Him. Aligning ourselves with God, communicating with Him at all times and in all situations and personal decisions will unite our hearts to His. A heart united to the Creator will overflow with graces and blessings.

Prayer and Spiritual Warfare: In addition, a healthy prayer life destroys strongholds that demons may have in our lives and in our hearts. Without prayer we cannot hope to be delivered from spiritual afflictions. It is no secret —prayer, worship, devotion, and living the Christ-Life in all that it entails is the formula not only for deliverance from spiritual afflictions, but for living the victorious life in Christ.

When dealing with spiritual afflictions, however, some special prayer considerations may be needed. Scripture states that there are certain demons that will only respond to prayer as well as fasting: *"But this kind does not go out except by prayer and fasting."* (Matthew 17:21). If fasting can defeat even the strongest of fallen angels, just how powerful is this sacrifice that we can make?

Spiritual warfare prayers are very effective in defeating the enemy and drawing our hearts closer to God.

Step 7 — Live the Faith and Remain Faithful

Along with all the advice and recommendations of the first six steps, our healing and deliverance cannot be complete unless we act upon our faith. Doing good works and charitable acts of love are a natural outflow of our faith and necessary to lead a good Christian life. It is not enough to believe. James asks and admonishes in James 2:19,20, 26:

Do you still think it's enough just to believe that there is one God? Well, even the demons believe this, and they tremble in terror! Fool! When will you ever learn that faith that does not result in good deeds is useless?

Just as the body is dead without a spirit, so also faith is dead without good deeds.

James calls a man a fool who does not act upon his faith in James 1:22-25:

Be doers of the word and not hearers only, deluding yourselves. For if anyone is a hearer of the Word and not a doer, he is like a man who looks at his own face in a mirror. He sees himself, then goes off and promptly forgets what he looks like. But the one who peers into the prefect law of freedom and perseveres, and is not a hearer who forgets but a doer who acts, such a one shall be blessed in what he does.

It is hard to live the Christ-Life, but we must try. We must not have a faith that is dead and useless. We must not be a fool and not practice our faith. We must, rather, live out our faith and persevere in the faith:

1 Corinthians 9:23-27

All this I do for the sake of the gospel, so that I too may have a share in it. Do you not know that the runners in the stadium all run in the race, but only one wins the prize? Run so as to win. Every athlete exercises discipline in every way. They do it to win a perishable crown, but we an imperishable one. Thus, I do not run aimlessly; I do not fight as if I were shadowboxing. No, I drive my body and train it, for fear that, after having preached to others, I myself should be disqualified.

Colossians 1:17-23

He is before all things, and in him all things hold together. He is the head of the body, the church. He is the beginning, the firstborn from the dead, that in all things he himself might be preeminent. For in him all the fullness was pleased to dwell, and through him to reconcile all things for him, making peace by the blood of his cross (through him), whether those on earth or those in heaven.

And you who once were alienated and hostile in mind because of evil deeds he has now reconciled in his fleshly body through his death, to present you holy, without blemish, and irreproachable before him, provided that you persevere in the faith, firmly grounded, stable, and not shifting from the hope of the gospel that you heard, which has been preached to every creature under heaven, of which I, Paul, am a minister.

And thus, let us be able to say, with St. Paul, in 2 Timothy 4:6-8

For I am already on the point of being sacrificed; the time of my departure has come. I have fought the good fight, I have finished the race, I have kept the faith. Henceforth there is laid up for me the crown of righteousness, which the Lord, the righteous judge, will award to me on that Day, and not only to me but also to all who have loved His appearing.

Persevere in the faith and let your life be a living Gospel for you shall thereby *"know the truth and the truth shall set you free"*

I have outlined steps detailing certain issues that we have found important in gaining freedom for a person in spiritual affliction.

1. purify one's conscience by a good confession;
2. Receive Holy Communion as often as possible;
3. Implore the mercy of God by prayer and fasting.
4. Recourse to specific spiritual warfare prayers applicable to the situation.

Final Thoughts

Repentance, forgiveness, acting on our faith, praying, fasting, receiving the Sacrament frequently, and all the rest we ought to do as good Christians are very good things and very necessary for this life, but more importantly for the life to come.

The advice contained in these Steps to Self-Deliverance, however, are not "quick fixes". This advice involves a lifelong commitment for anyone with spiritual afflictions. Freeing yourself from the bondages of the enemy and keeping them from returning requires this commitment to persevere in Christ and in the Christ-life.

There will be dry times. Your faith will be tested. Indeed, the demons may (and more than likely will) try to return. Scripture speaks of what demons do once they are cast out:

Now when the unclean spirit goes out of a man, it passes through waterless places seeking rest, and does not find it. Then it says, 'I will return to my house from which I came'; and when it comes, it finds it unoccupied, swept, and put in order. Then it goes and takes along with it seven other spirits more wicked than itself, and they go in and live there; and the last state of that man becomes worse than the first. (Matthew 12, 43-45).

Do not leave your house (heart) *"unoccupied, swept and put in order"*; rather be filled with the Holy Spirit.

We can never let down our guard. As a final instruction, remember the teaching of St. Paul in Ephesians 6:10-18. We do not go about our day without putting on our clothes. Do not go into the world with God's armor:

Finally, draw your strength from the Lord and from his mighty power. Put on the armor of God so that you may be able to stand firm against the tactics of the devil. For our struggle is not with flesh and blood but with the principalities, with the powers, with the world rulers of this present darkness, with the evil spirits in the heavens. Therefore, put on the armor of God that you may be able to resist on the evil day and, having done everything, to hold your ground. So, stand fast with your loins girded in truth, clothed with righteousness as a breastplate, and your feet shod in readiness for the gospel of peace. In all circumstances, hold faith as a shield, to quench all (the) flaming arrows of the evil one. And take the helmet of salvation and the sword of the Spirit, which is the word of God. With all prayer and supplication, pray at every opportunity in the Spirit. To that end, be watchful with all perseverance and supplication.

APENDEX 1
Steps for Self-Deliverance

The purpose of all this information is to enable you to do a self-deliverance at home for yourself. The process of self-deliverance is carried out in stages. Let's go through them one by one.

STEP ONE: Start with praise and worship. You can sing songs to praise God and to worship Him.

STEP TWO: Confess out loud Scriptures promising deliverance. Luke 10:19, Ephesians 1:7, Romans 16:20, Revelation 12:11, Colossians 2:14-15, Galatians 3:13-14, Psalms 91:3…_2 Timothy 4:18_ says And the Lord shall deliver me from every evil work, and will preserve me unto His heavenly kingdom: to whom be glory forever and ever. Amen. You should memorize _2 Tim 4:18_.

STEP THREE: Break covenants and curses to destroy their legal hold. You pray a simple prayer like this: I break any curse or covenant working against me, in the name of Jesus. (Simple prayers)

STEP FOUR: Bind all the spirits associated with those covenants and curses like this: I bind all the spirits attached or connected to the curses and covenants I have just broken, in the name of Jesus.

STEP FIVE: Lay one hand on your head and pray, Holy Ghost, cover me from the top of my head to the sole of my feet, in the name of Jesus. Begin to mention every organ of your body; kidney, liver, intestine, blood, etc. You must not rush at this level. Lay your hands-on areas that the Spirit of God leads you to.

STEP SIX: Then begin to saturate yourself with the Blood of Jesus. You do this by saying: I plead the Blood of Jesus over me. This must continue until you have a release in your spirit to stop.

STEP SEVEN: It is now, that you can demand firmly, in the name of the Lord Jesus Christ, that any spirit that is not of God should leave you. You demand it forcefully like this: In the name of the Lord Jesus Christ, I come against all you hidden spirits and I bind your activities in my life. You can no longer hide below the surface because I now recognize what you have been doing; release me, in the name of Jesus.

(If sickness is the problem, address it and say) You spirit of infirmity, I speak to you directly, get out of my life now. I am redeemed by the Blood of Jesus Christ, come out and go now. Go out with every breath by the power of the Holy Spirit. I prevail over you, in the name of Jesus.

STEP EIGHT: Ask for a fresh in-filling of the Holy Spirit and close the session with praises. Self-deliverance keeps you from getting sick; it removes every evil seed of the enemy; it charges your body with fire. It uproots evil plantations and builds up your confidence. Every night before you go to bed, you must remember these two important prayer points.

1. Pray for cover with the Blood of Jesus. **_Revelation 12:11_** = And they overcame him by the Blood of the Lamb, and by the word of their testimony; and they loved not their lives unto the death.
2. Pray that the Angels of God should surround you. **_Psalms 34:7_** = The Angel of the Lord encampeth round about them that fear him, and delivereth them.

No matter how sleepy you are, make sure pray these two prayer points every night. There is no reason why self-deliverance should not be effective. However, if the person seeking deliverance is under stubborn demonic control or hereditary strongman and lacks sufficient faith or authority to defeat the oppressors or living in any known sin, the evil spirits will be hard to get rid of. right.

 One final word of caution. For a person to be delivered, he/she must want deliverance. Self-deliverance must not be done because of pride, shyness, the fear of possible public embarrassment, etc. Your motive for engaging in self-deliverance has to be pure.

REMEMBER: **_DELIVERANCE IS A PROCESS (((NOT A ONE-TIME EVENT)))_** AND THE LENGTH OF TIME IT TAKES DEPENDS ON SEVERAL THINGS;

1. The length of time the spirit has stayed inside a person
2. The strength and reinforcement of the spirit
3. The experience and degree of anointing upon those who are ministering the deliverance
4. The willingness of the person being delivered to be free
5. The knowledge of the Word of God and your level of hatred for sin
6. SELF-DISCIPLINE IS NECESSARY

Also, remember that bondage can be weak or strong. A weak hold can be broken quickly, whereas a stronghold may take a more time. You will not realize the strength of bondage until you faithfully and persistently work on it. You must remember that a foothold can graduate to a stronghold if left unaddressed. After this exercise, set aside some days (with fasting). DO NOT CONTINUE TO DO THE THINGS THAT CAUSED THE "it"! CHANGE YOUR HABITS TO AGREE WITH YOUR PRAYERS. AMEN.

Appendix 2

Exposing the Doors to Bondage

Part I: The bondage

1. When did this bondage start?

2. Was there any unusual things that took place (or you did) when this bondage started?

3. If this bondage started when you were a child: Do you have ancestors who have suffered from a similar kind of bondage?

4. What kind of bondage are you facing? (Fears, depression, voices in your mind, mental illness, physical illness, mental torment, spiritual torment, etc... Please be as detailed as possible.)

5. What are all the things that have impacted your life? (Parent's death, trauma, a certain situation that changed your life, anything that 'changed' you.)

Part II: Your ancestor's background

1. Do you have ancestors who have struggled with similar problems or bondages?

2. Did your bondage start as a child and appear to have no reason to be there?

3. Do you have siblings who suffer from similar bondages or oppression?

Part III: Soul ties

1. Have you been involved with extramarital sex? Are you attracted to an ex-lover? Is he or she a good/godly influence for you?

2. Have you been divorced?

3. Do you feel an unusual attraction to a past boyfriend, girlfriend or lover (who is obviously not right for you)?

4. Do you let anybody dominate, control, or make your choices you?

5. Have you ever formed a blood covenant with another person? (Blood brothers, etc.)

6. Have you ever made vows or agreements with somebody in effort to strengthen the relationship or commit yourself to each other?

7. Do you see any ungodly relationships in your past where gifts were exchanged? (Are you holding onto something that was given to you from somebody you had adultery with, etc.)

8. Have you ever had ungodly relations with any one?

9. Do you have any pictures in your possession of somebody whom you may have an ungodly soul tie with? (A picture of you with somebody you had an adultery with, etc.)

Part IV: Relationship with parents

1. What do you think of your parents?

2. How would you explain your childhood?

3. Where you close to your parents while growing up? If not, why?

4. How would you explain your relationship with your parents? Was it good, bad or very cold?

5. Did you feel rejection from your parents?

6. Was either of your parents overly passive or controlling?

7. Has either of your parents been divorced? Remarried? Are your parents divorced?

8. How would you describe your relationship with your siblings growing up?

Part V: Rejection and abuse

1. Were your parents married when you were conceived? Were you the right sex? Did your parents not want you, or want you to be different (gender, etc.) in any way? If so, explain.

2. Did you feel rejected as a child? As an adult? If so, by whom? Explain.

3. Did you face abuse? What kind (emotional, physical, sexual, etc.) and by whom?

4. Have you faced rejection from your peers, classmates, friends or those around you?

5. Have you ever been put down, belittled, or made fun of? If so, by whom? Explain.

6. If you have faced rejection or abuse, how did you respond? Do you feel you are still paying a price for it? If so, how?

7. How do you respond to rejection right now?

8. Do you reject yourself (self-rejection)? If so, why and in what ways?

Part VI: Unforgiveness or bitterness

1. Is there anybody you feel edgy around? (Don't like them, feel anything in your heart against them, etc.)

2. Do you have anything against anybody? In other words, is there anybody that you have a hard time demonstrating the love of Christ to?

3. Has anybody wronged you that you haven't forgiven from your heart (thoughts, feelings, emotions, etc.)?

4. How do your view your siblings, parents, coworkers, etc.? Do you have any hard feelings against them?

5. Do you make a habit of blaming yourself for everything? Do you obsess over your mistakes and feel unusually guilty for them?

6. Do you deeply regret things that you've done in your past? Could you kick yourself over something you've done in your past? If so, explain.

Part VII: Personality

1. Are you a very positive or negative person?

2. Do you feel confident in yourself? If so, why?

3. Do you have a low self-esteem? If so, why?

4. Are you domineering or controlling? If so, to whom, and in what ways? Why?

5. Are you an achiever? (A go-getter) If so, in what ways?

6. Do you feel that you are always right and that if everybody did everything your way, this world would be a better place to live?

7. How do you treat your children? Husband? Are you controlling, passive, etc.?

8. Do you like people to 'look at you' (as in receive attention)?

Part VIII: Emotional health

1. Do you strive to feel accepted? If so, how does this affect your lifestyle? By whom do you want to feel accepted?

2. Are you always stressed out? If so, why?

3. Do you feel hurt? If so, by whom/what and why?

4. Do you feel good about yourself? If not, why?

5. Do you feel depressed? If so, why? When did it start? Did your parents or grandparents struggle with depression? If so, then do you know when it started and why? Do you have siblings who are also struggling? Do you feel your depression is rational or irrational?

6. Do you struggle with fears? If so, what is it that you fear? (Fear of heights, dying, being hopeless, failure, never marrying, etc.)

7. Do you worry about things? What things do you worry about? Why?

8. Do you struggle with anger? Do you have a short temper?

9. Do you have any insecurity? If so, explain.

10. Do you feel any self-pity or feel sorry for yourself? Have you ever felt this? If so, why?

11. Do you find it easy to hate people? If so, over what kinds of things would a person have to do to make you hate them?

12. Do you have any irrational feelings? If so, what are they?

13. Do you feel like something is wrong with you?

14. Do you feel excessively guilty over anything? Is this a continual problem?

15. Are you very confused and forgetful? (Beyond the normal)

16. Are you aware of any emotional wounds that have affected you?

17. Have you ever been deeply embarrassed over something? What was it?

18. Have you been in or are currently experiencing very difficult (depressing) circumstances which may cause you to feel hopeless or depressed?

Part IX: Who are you in Christ? And how do you see God?

1. How do you explain your relationship with God?

2. Do you feel you aren't good enough to meet His standards?

3. Do you see Him as a loving father, or a dictator?

4. Do you believe that it's only by the Blood of Jesus that your sins are forgiven? Or do you feel you need to earn your forgiveness in any way?

5. Do you feel God's love in your life?

6. Do you feel like your sins are forgiven? Or do you feel guilty?

7. Do you feel excessively guilty in everyday life?

8. Do you feel that doing good things, you earn God's love and acceptance?

9. Do you feel that God is angry or upset with you?

Part X: Spoken curses, vows & oaths

1. Have you ever spoken something negative about yourself that has come to past? For example: "I'm sick and tired..." or "If I don't quit typing, I'm going to get arthritis!"

2. Has your parents, or those in authority over you spoken out a curse over you? For example: "You'll never amount to anything!" or "You'll never get out of debt" or "You're so dumb"

3. Have you ever made a vow out of anger? If so, what? For example: "I'll never let anybody push me around again!" or "I'm never going to be hurt again!"

4. Have you ever wished to die? Have you ever said it?

5. If you have made any vows or oaths, what are they?

Part XI: Relationships

1. Do you have many friends? What kind of people are they?

2. Do you have a hard time trying to meet new people or make friends?

3. Are you socially outgoing or shy? If so, why?

4. How would you define your relationship with your spouse?

Part XII: Sexuality

1. Have you ever had unholy sex? What kind? (Fornication, adultery, sodomy, with a child, etc.)

2. Have you struggled with lust, fantasy or unholy sexual thoughts? If so, what kind?

3. Have you been attracted to pornography?

4. Do you have homosexual thoughts and desires? If so, have you acted upon those feelings?

5. How do you feel about your sexuality? (Do you feel dirty about it, or do you feel it's a wonderful blessing that God's given you?)

6. Do you withhold sex from your spouse or are you fidgety? Do you enjoy a healthy relationship with your spouse sexually? How does he or she react?

7. Have you ever been raped or sexually abused?

8. Have you ever woke up and felt a sexual presence with you? There are demons that imitate male and female functions, and stimulate their host (a person) sexually (beyond the normal 'wet dream').

9. Do you struggle or have you struggled with masturbation?

10. Do you struggle or have you struggled with any other sexual related thoughts, desires, or bondages?

11. Is there anything sexually that you are ashamed of?

Part XIII: Addictions

1. Do you have any addictions? If so, what kind? (Drugs, alcohol, smoking, eating, sex, TV, etc.) When did they start?

2. Did anybody else in your family (siblings, ancestors, etc.) have a struggle with any addictions? If so, what? Who?

3. Have you ever had, or currently have any sort of obsession over anything? If so, what?

Part XIV: False religions

Examples of false religions: Buddhism, Hindu, Jehovah Witness, Mormonism, Christian Scientists, eastern religions, etc.

1. Have you ever been involved with any false religions? If so, why, when and how long? How do you feel about those beliefs now?

2. Have you ever been involved in any secret societies such as Freemasonry? If so, how deep were you involved?

Part XV: The occult

1. Have you ever shown interest in the occult? If so, in what ways? (Read up on it, dabbled in it, etc.)

2. Do you still feel drawn or attracted to the occult?

3. Have you had any interest in horror or thriller style movies or novels? Are you still attracted to these things?

4. Have you ever made a vow with the devil? If so, what?

5. Married Satan?

6. Worshipped a demon or Satan?

7. Have you ever put a curse or spell on somebody?

8. Are you aware of any curses or spells placed on you? If so, what? Who did it?

9. Dabbled with an Ouija board? If so, why?

10. Ever been a member of a coven (group of 13 witches)? Explain.

11. Communicated with the dead? Explain.

12. Told somebody's fortune or went to see a fortune teller? Explain.

13. Ever read your horoscope?

14. Watched or been involved in a séance? Explain.

15. Have you been involved or a victim of Satanic Ritual Abuse (SRA)? Explain.

16. Been baptized into a false religion or any other evil baptism? If so, what were you baptized into? When?

17. Have you ever had a spirit guide?

18. Have you ever been involved with meditation, yoga, karate, or related activities?

19. Were you or anybody in your family superstitious? If so, who?

20. Ever been involved in astral travel? (Out of body)

21. If you have made any vows or oaths, what are they? Were there any sacrifices or rituals that were accompanied with them?

22. Have you ever made a blood pact before? If so, with whom (including persons, demons and Satan) and for what purpose?

23. Have you ever partaken in automatic writing, automatic drawing or automatic painting?

24. Have you ever been involved in Yoga, transcendental meditation, or similar activities?

25. Have you ever sought healing from a spiritual source other than Jesus Christ? (New age healing, energy healing, etc.)

26. Any other involvement in the occult? Explain.

Part XVI: Un-confessed sins

1. Are there any un-confessed sins that you have not repented of? (Usually something you've done, that you know is wrong, but won't admit to it. An abortion, stealing, etc. are some examples.)

2. Is there anything you've been hiding inside that you haven't confessed?

3. Do you feel excessively guilty over something(s) you've done in the past? If so, what?

Part XVII: Cursed objects

1. Do you have any idols, occult rings, or anything that could hold evil spiritual value in your home? If so, what? Any objects that hold evil spiritual value must be destroyed.

2. Do you have any gifts saved from sinful relationships? If so, explain. For example, if a man gives a woman a personal gift during an adultery that needs to be sold or destroyed.

Part XVIII: Severe trauma, abuse & disassociation

1. Have you ever been exposed to extreme abuse or a traumatic experience? Did it have a drastic effect on your emotional or mental system? If so, what happen? How did it affect you?

2. Have you ever disassociated or been diagnosed with Dissociative Identity Disorder (DID) or Multiple Personality Disorder (MPD)?

3. Are you aware of any alters (other personalities) that you may have? (If so, tell me about them)

4. Do you have a memory gap where you cannot remember a certain time of your life?

5. Do you have false memories of things that really didn't take place?

6. Have you ever been in a car accident or other traumatic situation? Have you ever witnessed a tragedy in real life?

Part XIX: Weaknesses

1. Do you struggle with any habitual sins? If so, what? Do you want to break those bad habits?

2. Do you struggle with any weaknesses such as lust, anger, hate, etc.? If so, what? Do you know where they came from or how they got started? Do you want to break free from those weaknesses?

Part XX: Pregnancy issues

1. Have you ever said something along the lines of, "I will never have children"?

2. Have you ever had an abortion or attempted one?

3. Have you ever had incest or ungodly sexual relations with somebody related to you? (See Leviticus 20:19-21, as this can cause a curse to land upon you which needs to be broken)

Part XXI: Other things to look for

1. Have you ever tried drugs? If so, how much, and how did it affect you? Why did you try drugs?

2. Have you ever thought about or attempted suicide?

3. Do you have any physical or mental disabilities, diseases or illnesses? Explain.

4. Do you want, and are willing to be delivered? Are you willing to give up those demon spirits and maybe make some lifestyle changes in order to keep your deliverance?

5. Do you experience unusual confusion settle upon you as you try to pray and read the Bible?

6. What kind of music do you like? (Please list all styles of music you currently enjoy, and give examples in each category you list, such as some names of artists and songs)

7. Have you previously enjoyed hard rock, metal, acid, alternative, rap, new age, or any other kind of worldly music? (Please provide some examples of artists and songs from each genre (type/style) of music you list)

8. Have you had any nightmares or weird experiences at night while supposedly sleeping?

9. Have you ever been in a trance or had an out of body experience?

10. Have you ever noticed time slipped right out from under you? For example, you look at your watch and its 7:00pm, then you look again what seemed like 15 minutes later and its 2:00am. This is a sign of a trance.

11. Have you ever touched or kissed a dead body? If so, explain whom and why and what happened afterwards.

12. Do you feel that you somehow have to earn your forgiveness? Do you 'wonder' if your sins are truly forgiven -- all of them? Are you aware of any signs of legalism or religious spirits operating in your mind?

13. Do you have any physical infirmities, sickness or diseases? If so, please list them.

14. Are you on any medications? If so, please explain.

15. Are you entertained by movies or TV shows which glorify death, murder, pain or suffering of others? Please explain.

16. Have you ever had any other kind of weird encounter with the spiritual realm?

Use this information to expose the root cause of the "it".

REFERENCES

1. Gary R. Collins, *Christian Counseling: A Comprehensive Guide*, 3rd Addition, Revised and Updated, NavPress, Colorado Springs, Colorado. ISBN 1418503290

2. Beilby, J.K. & P.R. Eddy. *Understanding Spiritual Warfare: Four Views*. Grand Rapids, Michigan: Baker, 2012.

3. Boyd, G.A., *God at War: The Bible and Spiritual Conflict*. Downers Grove, Illinois: IVP, 1997.

4. Hiebert, P. "Spiritual Warfare and Worldview"

5. Stedman, R.C, *Spiritual Warfare: Winning the Daily Battle with Satan.* Portland, Oregon: Multnomah, 1975.

6. Pirolo, N., *Prepare for Battle: Basic Training in Spiritual Warfare*, San Diego, California: Emmaus Road, International, 1997.

7. Arnold, E. C., *3 Crucial Questions about Spiritual Warfare*, Grand Rapids, Michigan: Baker, 1997.1

8. Rita Bennett, You Can Be Emotionally Free, 1982 ISBN 978 0 88270 748 8

9. Rita Bennett, Emotionally Free, 1982, ISBN 0 86065 194 0 Publishers, PO Box 777,

10. Tonbridge, Kent TN 11 0ZS, England, 1997, reprinted 2004). ISBN 1-85240-110-9. (Available in the US through the Arsenal Bookstore, 11005 Voyager Parkway, Colorado Springs, CO 80921.)

11. John and Paula Sandford, Healing the Wounded Spirit (Victory House, 1985). ISBN 0-932081-14-2.

12. Norma Dearing, The Healing Touch (Chosen Books, 2002). ISBN 0-8007-9302-1. Charles Kraft, Deep Wounds, Deep Healing (Servant Pub., 1993). ISBN 0-89283-784-5.

13. Derek Prince, God's Remedy for Rejection (Whitaker House, 1993). ISBN 088368-864-6.

14. Francis and Judith MacNutt, Praying for Your Unborn Child (1989). ISBN 0-38523-2829. (Available from www.Christianhealingmin.org, 904-765-3332.)

15. Thomas Verney, MD, The Secret Life of the Unborn Child (Summit Books, 1981).

16. Anderson, Winning Spiritual Warfare 1990 ISBN 13: 978-0-89081-868-8 James

17. Friesen, Uncovering the Mystery of MPD, 1997 ISBN 1-56819-062-7

18. Diane Hawkins, Multiple Identities, 2009 ISBN 978-0-9708073-6-6,

19. Restoration in Christ Ministries, http://www.rcm-usa.org/index.htm

20. Francis MacNutt, Deliverance from Evil Spirits, 1995, 0-8007-9232-7, Chap 17, pp 223-235 (best introductory material)

21. Daniel Ryder, Breaking the Circle of SRA, 1992, 0-89638-258-3 (an excellent book by a Christian counselor)

22. Margaret Smith, Ritual Abuse, what it is, why it happens, how to help, 1993, 0-06-250214-X (in depth information about SRA and MPD)

23. The Christian Bible

24. The following associations focus on trauma and disassociation www.sidran.org, www.issd.org

25. Pentecost, J.D., *Your Adversary the Devil.* Grand Rapids, Michigan: Zondervan, 1969

About the Author
Dr. Paulette Douglas

Dr. Paulette Douglas truly epitomizes elegance in living a saved, sanctified and Holy life, set apart from the secular world! Dr. Douglas is an ordained minister with the Pentecostal Assemblies of the World, an anointed national and international Evangelist, teacher and preacher. Dr. Paulette Douglas is renowned for the ministry of exhortation to the Body of Christ through deliverance, inner healing, salvation and biblical counseling at seminars, prayer clinics, crusades and conferences. She has established three churches and assisted in establishing many other churches, ministries and colleges as she serves on the Body of Christ for Jesus. Dr. Douglas was baptized in the name of Jesus Christ and filled with the Holy Ghost in 1977. She was called to the ministry in 1981, taught bible study at Pacific Bell for nine years which established the Radiant Life in Christ Ministries. She was the founder and pastor of the Radiant Life in Christ Community Church in Baldwin Park, California for nearly four years. Dr. Douglas retired in 1996 with full benefits from AT&T after 26 years of service. God introduced Dr. Douglas to the LOVE and HERO of her life, Bishop Robert T. Douglas Sr. They were married, the ministries merged, and she became the First Lady of the Jacob's Ladder Family, the Women's Ministry Director, the Church Executive Administrator and the Dean of the California University of Theology. Dr. Robert and Paulette Douglas are the proud parents of three wonderful children, Shakinah, Robert Jr. and Sondra Imani. They are also blessed with two granddaughters, Demi and Rob'Ann (butter ball) four grandsons, Dylan, Dominick Terrell, the twins Canden and Caden. Seven Godchildren and twelve God -grandchildren. Dr. Douglas is a graduate from Fuller Theological Seminary, Pasadena, California, Pentecostal Bible College, Ministerial Training Institute of Inglewood, California and Aenon Bible College West Coast. She has a Bachelors degree in Biblical Studies, a Masters degree in Theology, a PhD in Theology, Administration and a PhD in Biblical Counseling. She has earned certificates from California Christian Leadership of Orange County in biblical counseling, Zoe Christian Leadership Training Institute, Church Growth International, Seoul Korea and School of World Missions and Evangelism, Los Angeles. Dr. Douglas is formerly the Dean/Professor of the Inglewood Ministerial Training Institute of Inglewood, the Inland Empire Ministerial Training Institute, the Tri-County Ministerial Training Institute (San Bernardino, Riverside and Los Angeles counties) and the Living Waters Bible College, Rialto California. Dr. Douglas is presently the Dean of Colleges and Professor for the California District Council Aenon Bible College and Institutes, the Jacob's Ladder California University of Theology and Aenon Bible Institute CDC Extension Campus in Inglewood, California and the American College Theological Seminary International University (ACTS). All schools are fully accredited institutions for pastors, evangelist, teachers and anyone who has the call of God on their lives for ministry. Dr. Douglas is currently the CDC International Missions President and the past Church/Extension/Evangelism/Altar Director for the California District Council of the Pentecostal Assemblies of the World, Inc. Past Evangelism President for the CHDC Area 2 and has worked with the PAW Evangelism Ministry for more than 35 years. Dr. Paulette Douglas is the published author of the book series "Get Rid of It before It Gets Rid of You". Self-Help Instructions on how to correct and receive deliverance in every area of your life. Dr. Douglas portrays tremendous strength and endurance in the Lord by jointly sharing the vision and love for God with Bishop Douglas. Her primary objective in life is to be that "Excellent Woman of God, walking in His Divine favor.

Books and Recourses Compiled by
Dr. Paulette Douglas

"How to Get Rid of "it", Before "it" Gets Rid of You" Series (12 Books on Self Deliverance)

Volume One- Healing and Deliverance from Additions

Volume Two- Healing and Deliverance from Sexual Additions

Volume Three- Healing and Deliverance from Personality Disorders

Volume Four- Healing and Deliverance from Negative Relationships

Volume Five- Healing and Deliverance Through Spiritual Warfare

Volume Six- Healing and Deliverance from Negatives Attitudes

Volume Seven- Healing and Deliverance from Success Hindrances

Volume Eight- Healing and Deliverance from Tormenting Emotions

Volume Nine- Healing and Deliverance from Spiritual Weakness

Volume Ten- Healing and Deliverance from Salvation Issues

Volume Eleven- Healing and Deliverance from Domestic Problems

Volume Twelve- Healing and Deliverance Through Biblical Counseling

How to Have an Anointed Altar Workers Ministry

How to Have an Effective Prayer and Fasting Life

How to Walk in Your Grace as the Wife of a Minister, Deacon, Pastor, or Bishop

How to be an Effective Life Coach